Writing and learning

The NATIONAL *Writing* PROJECT

Nelson

Thomas Nelson and Sons Ltd
Nelson House   Mayfield Road
Walton-on-Thames   Surrey
KT12 5PL   UK

51 York Place
Edinburgh
EH1 3JD   UK

Thomas Nelson (Hong Kong) Ltd
Toppan Building 10/F
22A Westlands Road
Quarry Bay   Hong Kong

Distributed in Australia by

Thomas Nelson Australia
480 La Trobe Street
Melbourne   Victoria 3000
and in Sydney, Brisbane, Adelaide and Perth

©SCDC Publications 1989
First published by Thomas Nelson and Sons Ltd 1989

Photographs: Keith Hawkins (pp 6, 28, 52, 74, 77, 81, 90)
             Mike Levers, Open University (p 46)
             Alistair MacGregor (pp25, 26, 44, 56, 70)

ISBN 0-17-424112-7
NPN 9 8 7 6 5 4 3 2

Printed and bound in Great Britain by Bell & Bain Ltd, Glasgow

Acknowledgements

Hundreds of teachers and thousands of children have participated in the National Writing Project. They have been supported by many local advisers, members of higher education colleges, parents and others in the community. We cannot name them all, but we would like to acknowledge the commitment of those participants, and trust that these publications represent at least some of their views about classroom practice.

The National Writing Project was set up by the School Curriculum Development Committee. Its three-year Development Phase (1985-1988) directly involved twenty-four local authorities and it was funded jointly by the School Curriculum Development Committee and the LEAs. In 1988, the National Curriculum Council took responsibility for the Project's final implementation year.

Central Project Team (Development Phase 1985-1988)

Pam Czerniewska: Director

Eve Bearne
Barbara Grayson
John Richmond   } Project Officers
Jeremy Tafler

Naomi Baker
Anne Hogan   } Administrators
Judy Phillips

Central Project Team (Implementation Phase 1988-1989)

Jeremy Tafler: Director

Georgina Herring   } Project Officers
Marie Stacey

Rosemary Robertson: Administrator

Steering Committee

Andrew Wilkinson: Chair

Dennis Allen
Peter Andrews
Iain Ball
Douglas Barnes
Eunice Beaumont
Harold Gardiner
Alan Hall
David Halligan
John Johnson
Gulzar Kanji
Keith Kirby
Maggie Maclure
June Thexton
Jenny Taylor
Mike Torbe
Janet White

Local Project Co-ordinators

Avon	Richard Bates
Bedfordshire	Mary Heath
Berkshire	Audrey Gregory
	Barry Pope
Birmingham	Ann Davis
	Sylvia Winchester
Cheshire	Gill Fox
	John Huddart
Cleveland	Margaret Meek
	Joan Sedgewicke
Croydon	Sheila Freeman
	Iain Weir
Dorset	Barbara Tilbrook
	Margaret Wallen
Dudley	Chris Morris
Durham	Dot Yoxall
Gwynedd	Len Jones
	Esyllt Maelor
	Nia Pierce Jones
Hampshire	Robin Culver
	Cath Farrow
	Ann Heslop
	Roger Mulley
Humberside	Sylvia Emerson
ILEA	Helen Savva
Manchester	Helen Henn
	Georgina Herring
Mid Glamorgan	Richard Landy
Newcastle	Jay Mawdsley
Rochdale	Frances Clarke
	Peter Phethean
	Vivienne Rowcroft
SCEA	Stuart Dyke
Sheffield	Sue Horner
Shropshire	Ned Ratcliffe
Somerset	Vernon Casey
	Maisie Foster
	Carole Mason
Staffordshire	Sallyanne Greenwood
Wiltshire	Gill Clarkson
	Sue Dean
	Jo Stone

Contents

Introduction

Teachers involved in the National Writing Project in England and Wales have been investigating writing in their own classrooms. These materials, which include accounts of their investigations and examples of pupils' writing, are designed to help other teachers examine the ways in which writing can be used to promote learning. The accounts represent work in progress and are meant to stimulate discussion rather than to give prescriptions of how lessons should be carried out. They don't offer easy solutions to the everyday difficulties of developing classroom practices, but give honest accounts of the struggles and achievements of teachers and pupils. Perhaps most importantly, they raise issues which you may have encountered and which require resolution through discussion, negotiation, trial and error. The teachers were in the process of examining their own classroom practices when these descriptions of their investigations were written. They will have developed their practices and turned to new questions by the time you read their accounts — matters of culture, language variation and gender; of how to draw principles from classroom practice and work towards some ideas of what an effective writing curriculum should be. It is difficult to capture a process in printed form but we hope that readers will continue the teachers' process of critical investigation, using these accounts of work in progress as a springboard. Classroom organisation; curriculum and time constraints; intervention and response; purposes and audiences for writing are reflected as elements in the long-term process of developing a fuller writing curriculum.

Underlying the accounts in this pack is the assumption that writing can offer a unique means of capturing, considering and promoting knowledge. Set alongside the other language activities of talking, listening and reading, it is a central factor in learning.

Two questions teachers began with were: How can learning be made more effective? How can pupils be encouraged to take ideas and make them their own? These questions become particularly important when we want pupils to gather information from different sources, put it together and demonstrate in some way that they have, in fact, learned something. Very often, writing is used as a means of providing evidence that facts have been recorded or as some kind of proof that parts of the syllabus have been covered. It is a familiar experience, however, for teachers to feel that learning has at best been only partial. Equally familiar is the concern that when presented with material from books, fact sheets or television, pupils find it difficult to select relevant information and present it in a way which shows that they have understood what they have read, heard or seen. We may have taught, but how much have they learned?

The teachers' investigations into these questions are arranged in a progression, looking first at the individual's use of writing to stimulate thought and reflect on it, then broadening the view to look at classroom and wider school issues. Each section includes some comment from teachers who read and responded to draft material; these make further suggestions for activities or raise relevant questions.

Section One looks at how pupils can be encouraged to use writing as a starting point for learning — to gather ideas, organise, select and categorise them. Section Two extends this view of using writing to explore ideas by outlining ways in which pupils have been helped to reflect on their own learning.

Since these uses of writing thrive best in a supportive classroom environment, the accounts in Section Three reflect teachers' experiences of organising their classrooms as they attempt to introduce new ways of working. The importance of teacher collaboration and the difficulties which this might present are then considered in Section Four, before a review and summary of writing and learning draws the threads together.

Each of the sections includes accounts by teachers of different age groups and draws on experiences from different curriculum areas. This is a deliberate mixing, since teachers involved with the National Writing Project have emphasised the value of working with colleagues from different phases, sharing expertise and ideas. A short introduction and summary to each section outline the issues raised by the teachers' accounts. We hope that this book will provide some starting points for your discussions about writing.

Consultative Group

Eve Bearne
Sue Dean
Stuart Dyke
Cath Farrow
Maisie Foster
Audrey Gregory
Richard Landy
Carole Mason
Vivienne Miller

With thanks to all the teachers, children and parents whose work is represented here.

Special acknowledgement needs to be given to those teachers who responded to the early drafts of this material, in particular the trialling groups in Avon, Cambridgeshire, Gloucestershire, Hampshire, Haringey, Northumberland, Sheffield, Somerset and Wiltshire.

1 Learning through writing

Writing helps us to learn. We can work out ideas and reflect on them, record observations, capture and concentrate thoughts and so generate new ideas. How can we encourage pupils to develop a range of writing strategies which will help them through the learning process? How can they come to use writing for early planning, reflection and clarification of ideas? Just as new learning has to be supported by demonstration and chances to experiment, in the same way pupils have to be introduced to writing strategies which will help them make sense of learning activities. Classroom strategies which help learners to explore and make sense of their experiences through writing may involve shifts of perceptions about the purposes of writing. Rather than seeing writing as the automatic end point of any learning activity, teachers need to identify the different routes which can be taken when dealing with new ideas. This involves looking at how pupils may come to use writing to shape thought.

Often we don't acknowledge what we know until someone points it out to us. 'Thinking on paper' is one of the most effective ways for a learner to get to grips with what is to be learned. The first accounts describe ways in which existing knowledge can be recognised and made clear, and can form the basis for new experiences in writing and learning for children at the beginning of their school experience as well as those who are just reaching GCSE examinations.

Much classroom learning depends, however, on combining existing experience with knowledge which has to be taken in from a variety of sources, understood and made part of the learner's newly formed experience. Copying chunks of given material is a familiar feature of classroom writing. How can learners be encouraged to select relevant material, relate new information to what they already know and write it in a form which clearly demonstrates that they understand it?

What problems do teachers and pupils face when learning involves taking on new concepts, knowledge or practices? The final part of this section concentrates on ways in which writing can help pupils identify problems in their own learning, and on how they can use writing as a means of hypothesising and predicting. It focuses, too, on problems which teachers have identified in their classroom practice. These may be related to the content of learning, methods of presenting new ideas or ways in which writing may be more widely used to promote pupils' understanding. Making mistakes and working out how to overcome them is an essential part of learning. In this way, problems offer possibilities for development for both pupils and teachers.

Making learning visible

How to start off a piece of writing

Children come into classrooms with an enormous number of experiences and a great amount of knowledge about the world already stored in their heads. We think that helping them to tap into this source is a positive point for the development of their learning in school.

One strategy is 'brainstorming'. Brainstorming can be used for personal memories, information retrieval, ideas or questions at the beginning of a new enterprise, or as a means of reflection at the end to assess the work the children have been engaged

Inviting children to 'think aloud' on paper by using the strategy of brainstorming is a positive way of enabling pupils of all ages to acknowledge and draw on their own experiences, and in so doing, gain confidence as shapers of meaning.

in. A stimulus word is offered and the children are asked to catch any thoughts, ideas, information or memories that arise in association with the word. Words and phrases are jotted down randomly in a short burst of about five minutes. These initial ideas can be pooled with a friend, a small group or the whole class. The talk generates further ideas which can be added to the original list. The ideas can then be classified and used as starting points for pieces of writing or as ways into organising research — *'What do I need to find out?'*

The strategy can be used with very young children as a shared talk activity where the teacher scribes their ideas at the beginning of a topic or as a way into writing. It can be used with older pupils beginning a sequence of work for GCSE, to pool the knowledge the pupils already have and find out what they need to know.

In response to the question *'What do you know about food?'* one eight-year-old classifies her information as she brainstorms it.

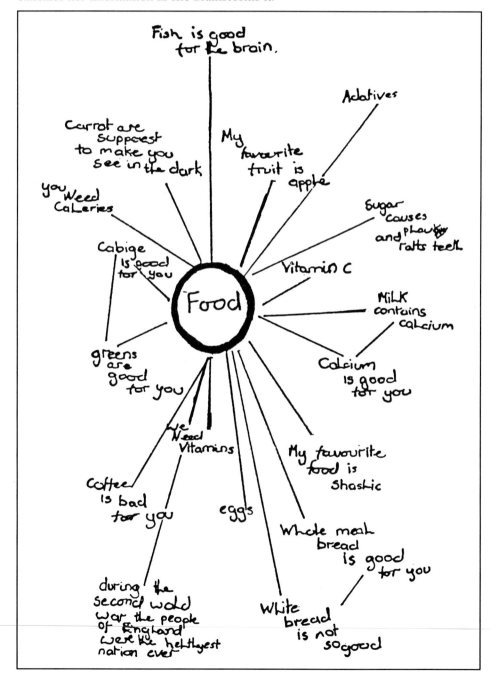

Winterslow Primary School

After talking about the story of St. George and the Dragon, seven-year-old children decided to write their own version of the story. Andrea brainstorms her ideas for the main characters.

Dragon
Fire breathing
Spikes
long powerful tail
Green
huge
Scales
Devil point on his tail
Sharp claws
four legs and paws
Meidum head big mouth
long red tounge like a snakes.
Walks like an elephant and eats them.

George
blond hair
Sceard of everything
didn't mean to kill dragon
lives in a shed
weighs 13 stone.
eats orange bubble gum
got plastic sword
loves animals
very weak.
Drinks and smokes
4ft tall
brown eyes.

Andrea
Princess
whars leather skirt and jacket.
Hates george
quite rich
lives in a thatch cottage
Tom boy
lashing mouth
Always get her own way
hates animals
short stricking orange hair
6ft tall.
Wishes to kill dragon before george

In preparation for writing a poem, later entitled 'Drowning memories', a fourth year Secondary boy brainstorms 'water'.

Winterslow Primary School

WATER

H_2O
Evaporation = Hydrogen + Oxygen
chemistry
Elba Panzer tanks went over the 12ft ice
cold
cleans
washes
drowns
pools, swimming lessons
sea, salt, Sodium chloride, chemistry, v. boring TV programme
take notes, forget to write up
wet

kettle, steam, burns, agony, wrist, 4 year old screams, cry, cry, cry
Hoes, fireman, fire in house 300 yards down the road
the burning inferno, movie, taped on video as soon as brother 19 started running it, mum burned of to watch program, when continued she did the same.

Jaws
Draught Devon can't pull chain   toilet stinks
Cool wet grass fire walking
PH7
100°c boiling point

Bishop Wordsworth's School, Salisbury

11

Such a strategy is valuable for a variety of reasons.

- It is a way of demonstrating to the children their capacity to retain words, ideas, visual images and information, and showing them what a powerful machine they have in their heads.

- It releases knowledge which the children did not know they had.

- It is a way of making the children their own experts. They can begin to see what they need to know, which can lead to real questions being asked and real research being developed.

- It takes the heat off the writing itself and puts it on to the learning. Words and ideas have the chance to tumble out without an emphasis on surface features, so that even the least confident writer can get ideas down on paper.

- It demonstrates that ideas do not emerge on to the page fully formed. Writers can think on to paper and then have the chance to develop or reject material as they find appropriate.

If we want children to be more in control, not only of their writing but of their learning, then brainstorming can usefully become part of their repertoire.

Sue Dean, Wiltshire Writing Project Co-ordinator

Puddles

Pauline Guy calls the initial process of drawing out ideas 'puddling'. She asks her seven- and eight-year-olds to draw a puddle, drop whatever they want into it, and see what splashes out. When they accidentally missed the third and final part of a television programme about a buzzard called Mordicas, she asked them to create their own endings, rather than simply telling them how the story was meant to end.

Organising initial ideas with seven- and eight-year-olds

Here is how one child 'puddled' her initial ideas.

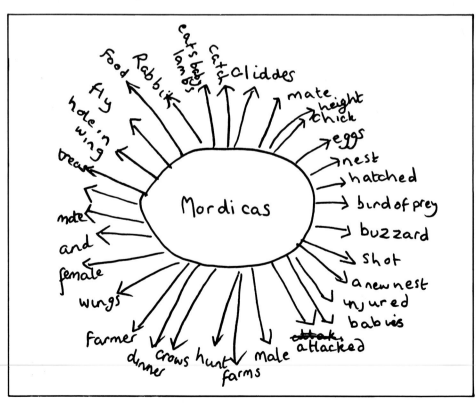

Story Plan
1. Mordicas is hatched
2. Mordicas grows up
3. Mordicas learns to fly and hunt.
4. Mordicas is injured
5. Hunting for a mate
6. His sisters take him away.

The ideas were then organised into a plan for the story, and the first draft of the story was written. . .

When Mordicas's mother and Father got some egg's and there was three eggs he pecked at his egg and he come out of his egg last When Mordicas's mother came home with food for mordicas his sister's took it of off him and that is why he was so small he was a buzzard bird.

... followed by the second.

Thursday 13th November
Mordicas is a buzzard bird and
he had just hatched he is
learning to fly and he fell
out of the nest and he found
a cardbord box and he hid in
it all throght the winter and
when he could fly he went to
hunt for a mate he found a
mate one day he was out hunting
he got shot on the wing and
he got very badly injured on
his wing but he can still fly
and he was very lucky
and he had to learn to fly
and he dh ad to lurn to glide
too he caught a Rabbit and
two crow's A guarding him
and he dropped the Rabbit
and he glided down and
got the Rabbit and the crow
swept down and Mordicas got
up in the air before
the crow got Back up in
the air.

From the original 'puddle' of ideas, the story is beginning to take shape. More discussion with peers and teacher will take place before the final version is achieved. Where weakness in sequencing occurs, the paper may be cut up and the pieces stuck down in a different order. Questions will be asked where something is not clear. Finally, the surface features, the spelling and punctuation, will be addressed and the final copy will be produced with attention paid to handwriting and presentation.

Pauline Guy, Oakwood First School, Southampton

Project planning in Computer Studies

A strategy for organisation with GCSE pupils

For many teachers, the introduction of GCSE and the compulsory assessment of coursework has caused a new set of problems. I am no exception. The WJEC Computer Studies syllabus states that the coursework project must be entirely the work of the student, with no intervention from the teacher at the planning stage. If I intervene in the planning process, the marks available to the students are automatically reduced. In addition to the other difficulties involved, quantifying my own intervention in the students' work may cause me something of a headache! I need to keep my intervention to a minimum while at the same time ensuring that the students plan their projects in a structured and coherent way.

The Computer Studies coursework project has to involve the solution (if possible) of a real-life problem. For instance, this might involve describing an existing work situation, looking at possible improvements and alternatives and explaining how the application of a computer package might assist things. Once this is done, the student has to produce some computer output to show that the problem can be solved or partially solved in this way, and to demonstrate knowledge of what the computer package can do.

Writing their accounts caused some students difficulties although, very often, they could give a perfectly clear oral account of their ideas and intentions. It was clear to me that the problem lay in the planning and structuring of the written work.

It was then that the potential of 'spidercharts' occurred to me. I remembered using them to plan my own work. Surely they could be used here? Students were asked to brainstorm a possible topic and then to structure a spiderchart outlining the ways in which computer applications might be developed for their particular problem. They saw the usefulness of this approach straight away.

They commented:
'This is useful — it makes sure we don't forget things.'

'It helps me to plan the order in which I write things.'

One of the good things about this way of working is that the ideas are generated very quickly and students are provided with an immediate way of demonstrating to themselves the potential of and the possible pitfalls in their chosen area of work. Also, it generates a useable written output which means that ideas and plans can be shared with other students. Most interestingly, many of the students eventually changed their topics, having worked out through spidercharts that their chosen subject had limitations which they had not foreseen.

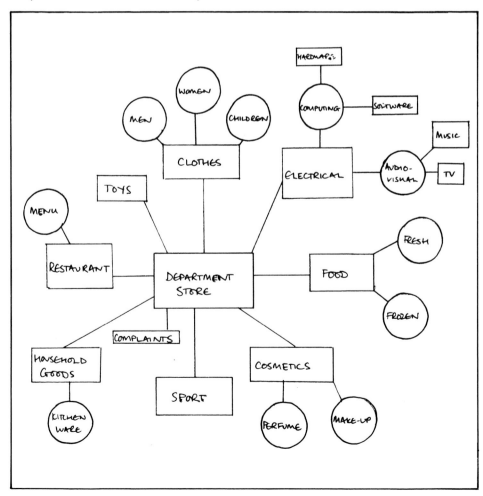

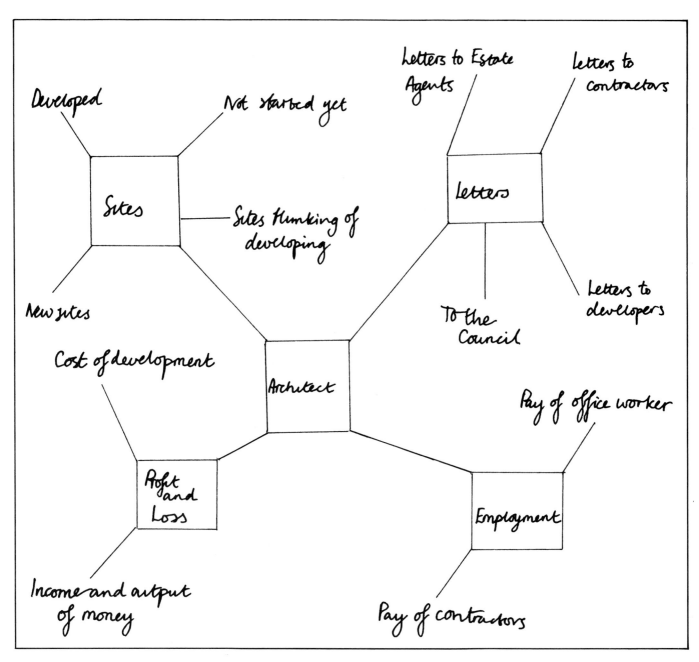

The examples illustrate some of the styles which were adopted. The main topic in each case has been subdivided into secondary topics which are themselves subdivided. Although there is some formal ordering, this graphical representation has another advantage in that it avoids the tendency to arrange ideas into an order of importance which may not be useful or relevant.

When they began their project work, many of the students were very apprehensive about what was expected of them, about the kind of writing they would be asked to produce and about whether this writing would satisfy the requirements of the GCSE examiner. The spidercharts do seem to have released the students from at least some of these fears and have helped to establish a real momentum in their work. What has really struck me about all this is the way in which 'disposable' writing can actually play a very important part in the exploration and structuring of work on a topic. Most importantly, this approach seems to have enabled the students to plan their investigations independently.

John Evans, Pencoed Comprehensive School, Bridgend, Mid Glamorgan

Teachers' comments

'Using puddling (I call it "webbing") has been a good way to help my very young children get their ideas out. Many of them speak a language other than English and some of them can write in different scripts, so I encourage them to do their webs in whatever language suits them. They talk to each other and to me about what they've written and get a lot of confidence from trying things out. We sort out their spellings later by using the word books, wall words and each other. It certainly does away with the fear of committing ideas to paper that I've seen in other children.'

'Brainstorming placed children in an organisational role and challenged them to organise their thoughts independently from the teacher. This strategy is useful throughout school and particularly useful for GCSE planning and revision work.'

'I like the strategy for planning and investigating a new topic and for reflection on a learned activity so that children can see what they have learned, to enhance their concept of their personal learning.'

'I tried to encourage children to write without asking me for words first time — interesting reactions, fear and frustration — the attitude of having a go at new words or trying to write without aid still needs to be fostered — the children will no doubt become more confident with time and encouragement from me.'

Looking at writing in the Humanities

First year Secondary pupils plan their research

The purpose of one unit in our Humanities course was to examine a group of people from the past and to attempt to understand their way of life and explain what motivated them to carry out a particular activity. The intention was that the pupils should empathise with these groups of people. Only two topics were covered, the first by the whole class, and one other as an option. The topics to choose from were:

Cave dwellers and why they painted on their walls

The Egyptians and why they decorated their tomb walls

The Minoan Cretans and why they decorated their palace walls

The last three accounts described strategies by which children can get their ideas out in the open to review and reshape them. Much classroom learning depends, however, on combining existing experience with new knowledge which has to be taken in from a variety of sources, understood and made part of the writer's newly formed experience. Ian Tanner describes how he found ways of giving the pupils in his History class the opportunity to produce a piece of extended writing from early notes and jottings.

We used prompt sheets to help pupils organise their ideas.

DANGER BEWARE! ROUGH PAPER

TITLE OF YOUR CHAPTER
☞

NAME
☞

WHAT EVIDENCE IS AVAILABLE?

BRIEF NOTES OF WHAT YOUR SECTION MUST CONTAIN

WHEN MUST THIS BE FINISHED
AND WHO DO I ASK IF I AM STUCK?

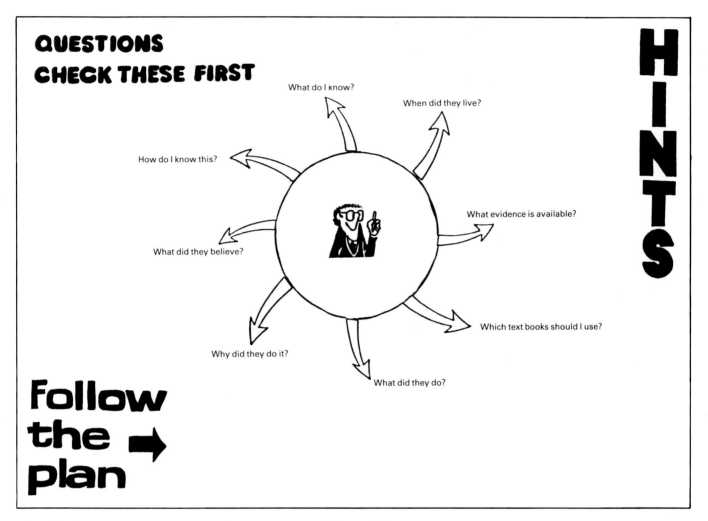

They also had text books as additional resource material if needed.

We discussed the questions on the sheet headed 'Hints' in relation to the first topic. Working clockwise around the questions, beginning with *What do I know?*, we showed that the pupils already had some useful knowledge and ideas. This activity proved valuable, giving pupils the opportunity to express their own opinions as to why cave dwellers painted their walls, and to discuss the ideas and dispute those which they considered to be implausible.

Making use of the topic theme sheet and rough paper, the writing process developed in approximately the following way:

1 Working in groups, the pupils researched the topic, using 'Hints', over a period of several lessons.

2 They replaced two of the questions with more specific ones related to the topic.

3 They decided who would answer which questions, ensuring that each member of the group answered at least two, using the topic theme sheet.

4 They consulted the textbook, making particular use of the contents pages and the index, and noted on their rough paper where they thought some answers to their questions could be found. They then read relevant sections and made outline notes.

5 Using the outline notes they wrote a detailed draft answer and checked this draft for both content and technical accuracy.

6 They decided upon a suitable form of presentation and wrote up the work as a complete answer to the original question.

The whole process took four lessons. I spent time helping those pupils who experienced difficulty in finding the information and constructing an answer, and I was able to give much more time to these pupils than when working in other ways. It has certainly provided a greater opportunity for extended writing within the History syllabus and has made us aware of possibilities throughout Humanities teaching in the school.

Ian Tanner, The Grange School, Shrewsbury, Shropshire

A return to Victorian values

A project in Brockmoor Middle School, Dudley, provided pupils, aged eleven, with the resources and opportunities to write extended fiction set in their home area during the Victoria era. For about six weeks the pupils, working in two groups of twenty-five, made their own models of Victorian life in the area: in factories, coal mines and the home. They also investigated the links between national events and local incidents.

Eleven-year-olds write historical novels

If children are to be encouraged to select relevant material, relate information to what they already know and write it in a form which clearly demonstrates understanding, they need to be motivated. Writing for a known audience helps to motivate the writer to take greater care with the planning, preparation and publication of his/her work.

As background to the novels we used sources such as old local newspapers and library services but the pupils demanded more specific information. One local library had a large and wide-ranging archive but the material was not easily available to children unless they were accompanied by an adult.

We overcame this problem by using 'A' Level History students from a nearby comprehensive school. The benefits that resulted were two-way. As the head of History from the comprehensive pointed out, it was ideal practice for his students who had to follow up lines of research dictated by someone else rather than following themes of their own choice. The 'A' Level students also visited Brockmoor to help our pupils sift through the material they had gathered.

At an early stage we visited the Black Country Museum to get the flavour of the period. Once the children had decided on an overall framework and some basic details we took them on visits where they were able to work individually on chosen aspects. As soon as we returned from these visits, many of the pupils would rewrite the drafts of early chapters so that correct factual information was incorporated into the narrative. For example, Joanne's slightly vague comments about a young woman's fear of the workhouse became:

'She fell and was badly injured and she is frightened her family will be put in the workhouse and she doesn't want that for the workhouse is terrible these days. It's under the Stowbridge Union and my Ma told me that the jobs they do are appalling . . .

On a Sunday afternoon when I take my walk I usually go past the workhouse. It's a stark place set well back off the Kingswinford Road . . . now and again ghostly white faces look aimlessly out of the barren windows and I always speed up my footsteps so as not to look for too long, it's a grim reminder of what life could be like if I were to lose my position here.'

We also brought in to the school visitors who had detailed knowledge of the area either through their own research or, where possible, through their own memories of the first part of the century. Arthur Willets, an expert on the local nail industry, spent a considerable time talking to pupils who were hoping to include references to this in their stories. There is no book on the subject and so direct contact was essential.

'Mrs Lucas started the fire up. It crackled and hissed like a snake, she then grasped a metal rod and thrust it into the fire, then clutched a hammer, her true strength

now showing. Harold began grumbling under his breath. I just caught what he said but unfortunately so did his mother. She clipped him round the ears, he shuddered and croaked . . .

As we worked the box in the corner gradually got more and more full as the pile of nails rose. Saturday would soon come and we had to get twelve thousand five hundred Brazil nails made or the nailmaster would close our business down. The Brazil nails had to be made crooked so that they'd be classed as unfinished items and the nailmasters wouldn't have to pay tax when they were shipped to South America.'

Many of the pupils also wrote about national events they had read of during the earlier research in order to retain authenticity if the narrative moved out of their home area.

'I soon reached Hyde Park and was greeted by the greatest sight I'd ever seen. The rumour about Crystal Palace was no longer a rumour, it was reality. Beefeaters stood at the gates in all their splendour, proudly wearing their red livery.

A huge fountain stood directly in front of me but it seemed to be frozen. On further examination I found that it was made of glass and wasn't real but the craftsmanship was so intricate it could have fooled anyone.'

There were frequent occasions when the pupils were able to help each other with background details or provide answers to specific questions. They were given complete choice as to the amount of drafting or early work before they arrived at the final version.

Georgina developed her final version from early jottings and notes:

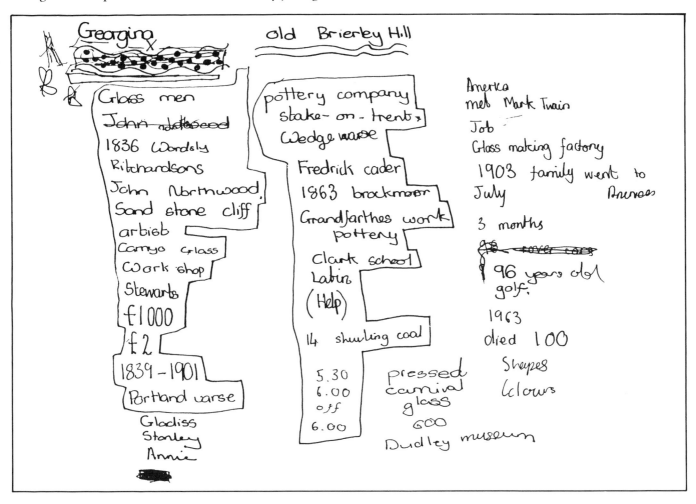

She revises as she writes, but after reading her narrative she makes further
alterations, adding descriptive detail to create atmosphere . . .

1900   In the morning   Book : Home Sweet Home
                                         Georgina Jones

I lay in bed, staring at the celling and the damp grey walls, which were dirty and covered with cracks.
A huge black cupboard was towering over me like a monster. I
turned over, and with an effort I pulled my white cotton shift over my knees.
I could hear the cry of Victoria in the next room. She's probably
cold again, poor kid. Then the bell rang. I quickly jumped out
of bed and I shivered as my feet touched the oil cloth. My shift was then flung off and drapped over
the iron bedpost. I slipped on my petticoat which felt harsh against my skin and ran
down the steps two at a time into the kitchen, where
I had to clean out the grate before we could
have any heat in the house. I then had to make
the fire by laying down screwed up paper, a few

. . . and including comments about her own feelings and emotions, blending these
with information about the period . . .

I slipped on my petticoat
which felt harsh against my skin, and
ran down the steps two at a time
into the kitchen where I had to clean out
the grate before we could have any heat in
the house and though my stomach felt
empty, I knew that I couldn't touch a
scrap of food until the fire was lit.* I
then ~~started to light the fire by laying~~
picked up an old paper and started to
screw it up until an advirtisment caught my
eye. It was a picture of a girl in a field
advatising Cadburys Choclate and her cat sat looking
longingly at her and thats just how I felt. my
insides were empty too* and with a brisk
~~down screwed up paper, a few sticks and~~
~~coal, and then I had to coax them to~~
~~life with a pair of bellows.~~
movement I threw the screwed up paper into
the grate, added some sticks and coal and
tried to coax them to life with a pair
of bellows. but still the fire would not
light. So I carried on trying for about five
minutes but still I had no luck. Then I
began to get my temper up and my hair
kept falling down from under my cap.

After further discussions with her teacher and friends she decides on the final version.

I slipped on my petticoat which felt harsh against my skin, and ran down the stairs two at atime into the kitchen where I had to clean out the grate before we had any heat in the house and now my stomach felt empty, I knew that I couldn't touch a scrap of food until the fire was lit.

I then picked up an old newspaper and started to screw it up until an advertisment caught my eye.   It was a picture of a girl in a field advertising Cadbury's chocolate and her cat sat looking longingly and that's just how I felt my insides were empty too.

Then with a brisk movement I threw the screwed-up paper into the grate added some sticks and coal and tried to coax them to life with a pair of bellows but sill the fire would not light. So I carried on trying for about five minutes but still I had no luck. Then I began to get my temper up and my hair kept falling down from under my cap.

When a writer was happy with a chapter, it was typed out by the teacher, the headteacher or a pupil. Illustrations from a wide variety of sources were often included.

After two terms writing their own fiction set in the period, the pupils really did know something of what it was like to be Victorian. Throughout the work, they set their own questions to be answered to improve their own stories. Proof that the pupils assimilated the real meaning behind the answers to their questions is that the stories never become technical or information-orientated but conveyed the atmosphere suggested by the research.

'My comb was harsh on my head as it scraped my scalp. I glanced at the clock which was half past five. I must get to work. I left my attic where I had lived for the past two years since I was ten years old when my mother got me into service. I tiptoed past Mrs Pines' bedroom and went downstairs. I opened the kitchen door. No one was about, the fire had not been lit but it was still warmer than my room because the last embers of the fire had probably struggled till dawn.'

When politicians next call for a return to Victorian values, perhaps these writers will question exactly which values they mean.

Linda Whittall, Brockmoor Middle School, Dudley and Chris Morris,
Dudley Writing Project Co-ordinator

This approach drew on the community as a rich resource and as an audience for writing. Through detailed observation, listening and recording, other pupils have been able to recognise the hidden histories of their families and community. Teachers in the Dudley Project found that their work on researching histories followed a similar pattern. The diagram indicates the processes involved and the variety of outcomes.

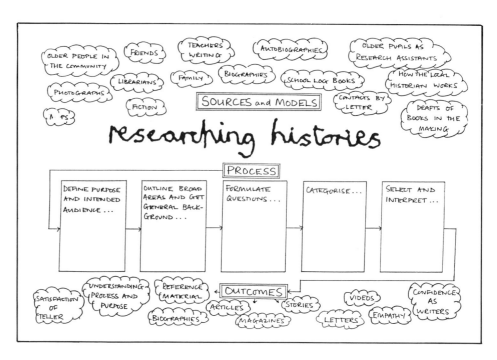

For discussion

The process outlined in the diagram offers a framework for planning in other subject areas. The skeleton diagram could be used as a basis for designing a series of activities either with your own class or as a joint planning framework with colleagues.

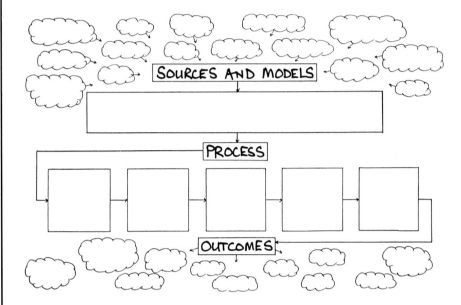

One teacher used it to plan a book writing exchange:

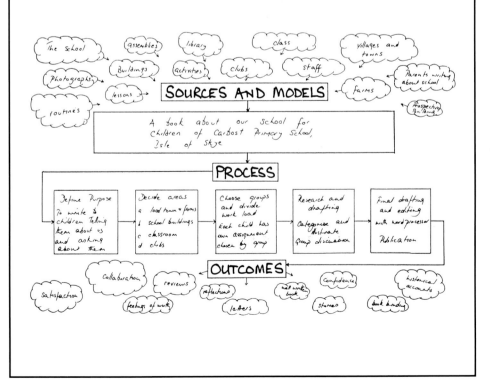

Teachers' comments

'As a history teacher I'd never thought of combining fiction writing with researching community history — although there's now a great emphasis on empathy writing, particularly in GCSE. I'm excited about these ideas. Using local archives and, in my case, family histories, means that we can tackle those areas which have been 'written out' of many history books — women's experience; women as important figures in history (they often feature in local archives and census material) — and using fiction as a medium allows the boys, too, to "step into other people's shoes" . . . '

' . . . I've had my eyes opened. I now see myself as a teacher of language and history . . .'

'One experience I want my pupils to have is that of writing a poem that requires initial planning and/or research. I want them also to look at and understand stereotypes and the kind of unthinking assumptions that we all sometimes make. One purpose of carrying out research in order to write a poem is that it doesn't require gathering masses of information. Pupils do, though, have to judge what they want to know, when they have enough information and how they will use it. Research and experience make it clear that it is easier to gather information when you know why you want it.'

Problems and possibilities

Writing in Mathematics

Teachers in Mid Glamorgan Primary and Secondary schools have been trying out different ways of using writing in Mathematics. Their discussions are summarised here.

WRITING IN MATHEMATICS

SOME PROBLEMS ...

RELUCTANCE

Sometimes there is a reluctance to write in what has traditionally been a 'non-writing' subject.

CONFUSION

Pupils can become confused between 'longhand' writing and elegant mathematical shorthand. Does the writing necessarily distract from the Maths?

SEPARATION

There can be a problem when the TALKING that's an essential part of learning in Maths doesn't relate to the WRITING that's done.

IRRELEVANCE

Maths sometimes appears to exist in a vacuum and is seen as 'abstract' and divorced from everyday activities - including writing.

UNCERTAINTY

Sometimes pupils aren't clear about the FORMAT in which they can most usefully write. Hence, the fear of putting pen to paper.

... AND SOME POSSIBILITIES

VARIETY

Opportunities for writing in various formats - journals, reports and stories. At its best, writing can explore the meanings of mathematical principles.

AUDIENCE

Opportunities to write for different groups and individuals, other than the teacher, to explain or clarify, providing information or guidelines for others.

COLLABORATION

Pupils in pairs or in groups, working with each other in order to make the move from talking to writing less sudden and more meaningful.

REALIZATION

Making the Maths REAL - giving it practical applications. There are many ways in which writing can help to give the work a 'real' context.

INDEPENDENCE

Opportunities for pupils to use writing to develop their own researches and investigations, making their own original contribution to the group's work.

CLARIFICATION

Making the learning that has taken place explicit - providing a space in which ideas can be sorted out and in which pupils can ask the questions they need to.

EXTENSION

Opportunities to EXTEND ideas and to develop them further - providing a chance for pupils to hypothesise and to try things out.

Scratch pads

Juniors write about learning Mathematics

Neil Griffiths describes his own Primary school experience as resulting in the three Fs — frustration, fear and failure. His aim in teaching was to help children to be confident, positively engaged and enjoying their Mathematics.

I am sure that every teacher in the land must have said at some time or other, *'If only I had more time and fewer children. I just can't get to see them all.'* I was faced with such a problem; thirty-five fourth year Juniors and the impossible task of trying to track, record and follow up thirty-five interweaving threads of thought, understanding and learning.

Marking their books was a poor substitute as I have always felt it is vital that the child is present in order to explain and talk through ideas and methods of working. This was not always possible and the time lapse between completion and the marking of work meant that the children often lost the thread of their thoughts. I wanted to provide the children with a regular, constructive and consistent response partner, and scratch pads provided a useful alternative. It gave the pupils the opportunity to use their notebooks to reflect, clarify, note-take, illustrate and present data, define, explain, give opinions and summarise their work.

The pads were a sounding board for the child, a line of communication between teacher and pupil. They provided me with a 'window' into the child's mind and, perhaps of greatest significance, the children's writing was being used to shape meaning, reflect upon thoughts and clarify understanding.

At first the children were unsure about how to use them. They gave guarded responses and it was obviously important to build up a relationship of trust between teacher and pupil. Every response in their books was seen as a valuable one, and whenever possible a reply would follow.

Initially I asked the children to use the pads to reflect on certain lessons or some aspect of the work they were involved with. Comments were typically tentative:

'The Maths was boring.'
'I kept getting stuck.'
'I liked our work today.'
'It was easy so I liked it.'

In an attempt to encourage greater confidence I responded in writing, offering open-ended questions inviting the children to write back. Gradually their reflections developed:

'It was the long adding up that let me down.'
'You went too fast giving out your instructions.'
'I wish I knew my eight and nine times tables!'
'The toy animals helped because I could see what was happening in the sets.'

I am carefully selective when using scratch pads, always encouraging the children to write if they have anything on their minds, which they may or may not wish to share, but only directing when I feel there is positive value or feedback to be gained. The pads are always present during Maths lessons as it is vital for them to be accessible, but they are not always written in.

The scratch pads often provided me with an invaluable insight into what they knew or didn't know when embarking on a new concept. I might ask what they understood by the term 'average' or 'angle' and the pupils would attempt to give a definition. For example, responses to the question *'What is an angle?'* were most revealing:

'Two lines which joined at a point.'
'A corner.'
'A space between two lines.'
'A protractor makes them.'

The scratch pads provided a useful picture of where I needed to pitch my starting point. I asked a fourth year group why we were doing work on subtraction. They believed it was:

'To please you, sir.'
'Because we have to take away all the time in school in Maths lessons.'
'So that we don't get behind at Secondary school.'

Their feelings and honesty had an impact on my own thinking, and I was moved to spend more time discussing with the children not just the 'hows' but also the 'whys' of Mathematics.

After a year of working with one fourth year group, the development and greater maturity of thinking is evident. I asked a similar question relating to decimal work. Some responses were:

'Money is a decimal system and we use money all the time, so it's important.'
'We understand how they work.'
'Some decimals are fractions, .5 is $^1/_2$, .25 is $^1/_4$ and they are used in everyday life.'

'I have seen decimals being used in ice skating. 5.9 means nearly 6. 6.0 is a perfect score.'
'Measuring in centimetres, metres and kilometres is a decimal system and it makes life much easier.'

It is only now, after a year of using the pads, that the children have the confidence and sense of security to offer honest opinions, which provide invaluable insights not possible in normal classroom contact time. They save precious time which was wasted in the past on recording pages of answers. Perhaps one of the most pleasing responses was given by a fourth year girl who provided me with this definition of the term 'average':

'An average is about the middle value. It is a good guide to how many you are likely to get in a box of Smarties or matches. You may have a few more or a few less. To find an average you add up every individual total in each box and divide by the number of boxes. This gives you the average content.'

Such a definition indicated a full understanding of the concept of an average and proved she knew how and when to use it. No need for endless pages of recording, and example after example.

I hope I have not presented the view that it is only the teacher who benefits from the use of scratch pads by seeing the child's train of thought. Indeed its greater potential is the opportunity it gives the children for using writing to shape meaning, and to capture and crystallise their thoughts. For so many children a point of frustration is reached when they have understood a concept, only to find they are unable to put it into words.

Having successfully used scratch pads for over a year we are now at the stage within the school where they are to be introduced to all the children in the Junior section and they are to partner each of the pupils' workbooks. Although many of the staff are still tentative and I am aware that they too need to go through the stages that I experienced, it is clear to us all that the children's confidence, perseverance, enjoyment and understanding of Mathematics have undoubtedly changed as a result of their use.

Neil Griffiths, West Lea Primary School, Wiltshire

A fuller account of Neil Griffiths' work appears in a Wiltshire 'Write to learn' Project booklet 'Ssh! It's a Maths lesson.'

Thinking, learning, writing

Writing in Secondary Science

All learners and writers bring to each task the paraphernalia of what they already know, think and have experienced. This affects their view of where they are going and why they began, and of the conditions under which they are operating. In order to grasp new thoughts, ideas, emotions and experiences, learners need to explore the meaning, limits and significance of these and to discover how the new relates to the known.

This has much in common with the view of learning as conceptual change, which is the basis for the Children's Learning in Science Project based at Leeds University. This project suggests four areas which must be taken into account when designing learning materials and situations. Two of these, content and teachers' practical knowledge of students, schools and classrooms, are commonly part of planning the curriculum, but the other two areas, information on pupils' prior ideas and perspectives on the learning process, are not acknowledged so often. If these are

Learning in any curriculum area often follows similar processes. In this description of a Science project, the initial framing of experiences and knowledge that pupils brought to the topic formed a basis for their investigations where writing helped them to establish starting points as well as to predict, hypothesise and draw conclusions.

ignored, then the teachers' practical expertise and the relevance of the content are in danger of being rendered less effective. The teachers' expertise in classroom management is wasted if the ways in which pupils learn are not clearly in view. The relevance of content depends on what pupils already know, or want to find out.

Writing has the merit of making explicit and visible things the writer understands:

- if I already know, then I can confirm that

- if I'm not sure, then I can try it out and see whether it looks as though it works

- if I am confused, then maybe some jottings will clarify the issues

Talking can also do all these things, but the visual aspect of writing and hence its permanence as a record offer opportunities for me to inspect what I think more closely and at a larger distance than oral expression allows. Writing also allows for more detailed reconstruction, adjustment, finesse.

Writing can perform many functions but in schools it tends to be relegated to the end of the learning process, and this not only narrows the learner's view of writing but also may hinder the other processes which are involved in learning. Writing may be used for interim, exploratory purposes as well as for a final statement.

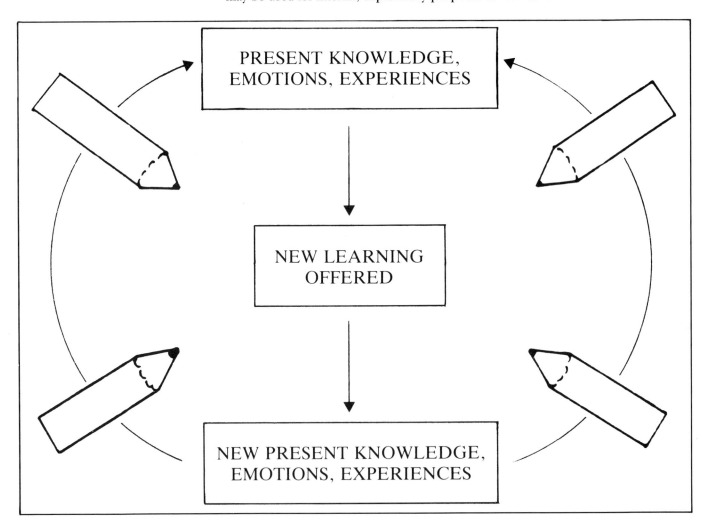

PRESENT KNOWLEDGE, EMOTIONS, EXPERIENCES

NEW LEARNING OFFERED

NEW PRESENT KNOWLEDGE, EMOTIONS, EXPERIENCES

Learning is not a single operation. It is a range of activities and strategies which enable the learner to categorise, analyse and organise new material, and perceive relationships both to previous understanding and within new understanding. In the course of this analysis and organisation the learner may predict, hypothesise, visualise, empathise and imagine.

Learning is thus internalised and may then be transferable, no longer restricted to the original context in which the new understanding was found. Learners engage in these activities across a wide range of situations, whether they are writing a novel or testing racing bikes.

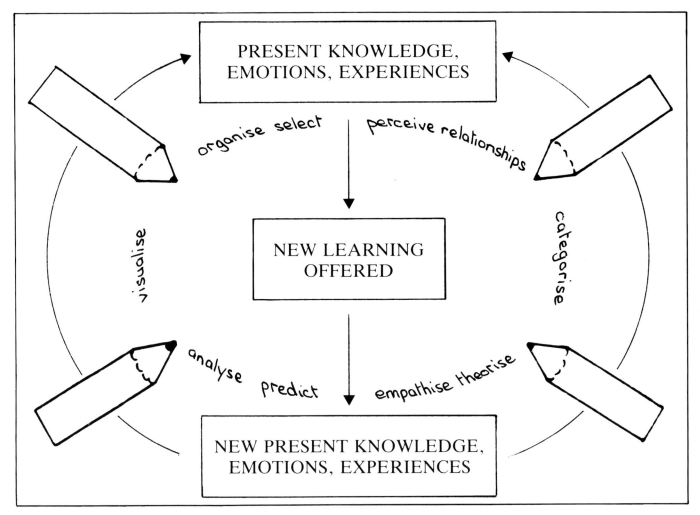

Many of the activities in the diagram may also be achieved inside the learner's head, without any external expression, written or oral, once a competence has been acquired. But we all need to talk or write about some of our new ideas or experiences before we fully understand them. The most convincing evidence of learning having taken place is when the learner is able to predict on the basis of new scientific knowledge or empathise with a character in a novel, rather than replicate the original information or merely give an account of what happened to the character.

In a series of Science lessons with a group of twelve- and thirteen-year-olds, we tried to embody some of these ideas in classroom organisation and lesson structure.

With regard to Science, our aims were:

- to make explicit what pupils already know about the topic
- for pupils to identify which lines of enquiry they would like to follow
- for pupils to test their own hypotheses
- for pupils to evaluate and present their thinking and their work

With regard to writing, we wanted:

- thinking processes to be reflected in the writing

- pupils' writing in Science to be given status through display

- writing to be in a form chosen by pupils

The topic for the lessons was 'breathing', about which pupils had some prior knowledge, certainly experientially and also in other contexts in Science.

The lessons happened in the following sequence:

1 Working in groups, the pupils listed anything they could say about breathing.

2 They tried to agree on a definition of breathing. This was intended to help them to begin to assess which were the essential points in their list.

3 The pupils then looked at the list and decided which of the statements about breathing could be tested empirically and which would have to be researched in books. Testing whether air goes directly from the lungs to the brain would be impossible, whereas testing whether chest expansion correlated with lung capacity was a feasible enterprise in the lesson.

4 Pupils wrote on a sheet the statement they were going to work on. They then turned the statement into a question.

5 Before beginning the practical work, they wrote down what they were going to do and what they thought would happen. This was to enable them afterwards to be able to assess their hypothesis in the light of what actually happened.

6 Pupils carried out the practical work. These sessions were lively since so many different experiments were going on.

7 The pupils devised a display to present what they thought, did and found out.

8 When the displays were ready the pupils explained their work orally to the rest of the class. In this session the range of activities undertaken became evident and pupils asked each other questions about what they had done.

9 The final activity was to go back to their original definitions of breathing, which had been displayed around the room, and to decide whether they thought these definitions were satisfactory or if they should be modified in the light of the work done.

While some pupils chose to do experiments with which they were already familiar, others set out to make new discoveries. One pupil wanted to find out whether plants breathe as humans do by trying to suffocate a plant. The plant survived and the writing that accompanied the presentation was not only direct, but dramatic:

'The plant lived for the first day,
and the plant lived for the second day,
but on the third day the plant started to sweat.'

This experiment led to a discussion which introduced scientific concepts that the teacher would have considered too difficult for this pupil had not the initiative and need to know come from his own interest.

The writing the pupils produced was in their own words and for some pupils it also reflected their thinking:

'In theory we thought . . . This proved right for most . . . but some of us were different.'

Although they were not using a traditional format for their writing, they organised the content logically and clearly. The invitation to display their work led to the investment of much care and effort in presenting their findings in as impressive a way as possible. This sequence of activities, then, provided some evidence of the feasibility of enacting the relationship between thinking and writing in lessons, and of the value of a process which begins with the pupils' existing knowledge rather than consisting solely of what the teacher wishes them to learn.

Sue Horner, Sheffield Writing Project Co-ordinator, with thanks to Julia Cooke, High Green School, Sheffield

Teachers' comments

'I like the idea of getting children to ask questions before or during Maths work. My own experience of Maths at school was confused. I'm sure I'd have been able to succeed if I'd been able to ask the questions I needed to ask.'

'What I want to do now is to look at the different ways in which boys and girls write in Science. I've looked carefully at the work we did last year and it may be just an impression — I think there are differences. Perhaps a more open approach like this will help. I've often noticed, for instance, that in mixed groups the boys do the "work" and the girls do the recording, and I've already tried to find ways of dealing with that by insisting that everyone has a chance to do some of each.'

'We have recently become interested in using writing in our Maths problem-solving work. We began by asking pupils in lower Secondary classes to write up what they had done. Writing up in this way provides evidence of the investigative process the pupil has undergone, and misconceptions or incorrect processes can be identified and corrected. One of the most important stages of an investigation is the final assessment by the pupil of their investigation and the report provides a vehicle for this. Because this proved so valuable we decided to change the focus of the writing. We encouraged pupils to write as they progressed through their investigations, rather than leaving all the writing to the end. Eventually, we aim to develop pupils' ability to use their investigative skills to tackle and develop an investigation independently and as they see appropriate. This will be different for each pupil, and so the style and form of the written work should also be of the pupil's choosing and appropriate to the investigation.'

Summary

All the accounts in this section offer ways of using writing to help learning as it is happening as well as, at times, using writing to communicate what has been learned. They emphasise that:

- by using writing for preparation, to get ideas out in the open and then take a critical look at them, learners come to see that they can use writing for their own purposes

- planning strategies and frameworks, and methods for reorganising early drafts or for categorising information all add to children's knowledge of how language can be shaped to fulfil their own intentions, to make their own meanings clear

- in researching a particular topic these strategies offer a focus for learning, helping the learner to decide where to go next in gathering information

- when writing is seen by teacher and pupils as a means to an end as well as an end in itself, it becomes easier to identify areas where extra help is needed or where significant progress has been made

- drawing attention to what the learner already knows and can do, provides a strong base for future learning

- taking time over writing, talking about it and revising it encourages children to be more critical readers of their own writing and to find ways of improving the content, organisation and technical accuracy of their work

- rather than being seen as a means of judging success or failure after a learning activity, writing can be used as a way of contributing to the continuing process of learning

- the teacher's role is crucial in introducing and demonstrating these techniques for organising learning and in offering clear explanations of the purposes of different learning strategies

2 Reflecting and responding

By seeing that writing can be changed, reorganised and developed, often alongside discussion with others, pupils will be more able to decide the best means of using writing for their particular purposes; they will have available a range of resources and techniques for handling a variety of tasks. The previous section outlined some of the strategies which pupils can bring to bear on learning. This section describes further ways of using writing to explore and extend ideas, and then considers some of the consequences.

Writing often results in some action. We use lists as a prompt for doing things and get satisfaction from crossing off items when we've completed tasks. If we write a letter we look forward to the reply. Often we show early drafts of more considered pieces of writing to someone so that their response will confirm our ideas or help us to express them more clearly. We may resent time spent on writing an account of a meeting or activity if no one takes any notice of it. We expect writing to be read by someone, if only ourselves, and anticipate some kind of response. How do these expectations match with pupils' perceptions of writing in schools? And how can teachers encourage pupils to read and write for meaning as well as for technical accuracy?

The traditional response to classroom writing is often a mark or a grade and some correction of technical errors. What are the consequences of this for learning? One consequence may be a mismatch between the teacher's view of the purpose of any activity and the pupil's perceptions of the task. Reflective writing can be a way of creating more common understanding of what learning is about. It can be used as a means of genuinely informing teachers about children's learning as well as helping pupils to reflect on what they have learned, establishing some kind of dialogue.

There are sometimes fears that introducing ways of writing which need considered response from the teacher will result in an extra workload. This can, of course, be the case although the teachers' accounts which follow suggest that the benefits outweigh the disadvantages.

I can scream and shout without making a noise

Fourth year Juniors keep Maths logs

I began using journals in Mathematics with my class of ten-year-olds with several aims in mind. I was aware that the children were finding it difficult to articulate their difficulties with the subject and to explain their problems to me. Questions such as *'Why did you write that?'* or *'Can you explain this?'* tended to precipitate a state of shock. So I was looking for a means to aid learning and understanding while at the same time providing an opportunity to reshape attitudes and build self-confidence. Above all, I was anxious to dispel the tensions and fears that surround Maths for so many children.

Despite genuinely trying to make Maths lessons relaxed and rewarding, I knew that they were too often a time of trial and tribulation for us all. So when our local Writing Project group began to consider the possible uses of journals in different

Writing is for reading — by ourselves and others. We can capture our thoughts and feelings so that we can reflect on them later or use our reflections as a basis for both spoken and written dialogues. The following account shows just how powerful writing can be as a means of shaping and changing ideas for pupils and teachers alike.

areas of the curriculum I jumped at the opportunity to try them out in Maths.

Most of our Maths sessions are in the mornings and about twice a week the class uses the last fifteen minutes of a lesson to write in their journals. Sometimes I will suggest a topic to them but the children are always free to comment on their work that week, to express their difficulties and understandings, to make suggestions and to ask questions. Sometimes they will explain what they have been doing to another member of the group. Their written explanations seem to help them with their own insights. Perhaps I should mention that I was, myself, no mathematician at school. Like most others I relied on the use of arithmetical 'tricks' which didn't always work. Certainly a genuine understanding of the concepts involved eluded me until I actually began to teach them. I think it's true to say that the children's reflections on their own learning have helped them to gain a greater awareness of mathematical processes.

The children reacted positively to the idea of keeping a Maths journal. There was great enthusiasm to put pen to paper and the results in turn amused, delighted, informed and chastened me.

Many of the children chattered away in a very friendly tone:

Until today, I thought that multiplying fractions was easy. Now I realize it isn't. God help me when I do algebra!

When I first came to school this morning, I was cold. But as the morning went on, I got warmer this helped me to do maths. I was glad when playtime came.

Nichola

> I would also want to know If you mak our work like this my capabilitys or my speed or my neatness or all of them. I also got stuck when I have to simplifie before multiplying fractions.

Stuart

I reassured Stuart and the rest of the class that I would not be correcting the spelling and other surface features of their writing, but that I would try to respond to what they had to say.

Some of the children who found Maths very difficult were among the most willing to communicate and they certainly didn't seem to be afraid to write about a subject in which they needed a great deal of support and encouragement.

> I Dont understand Fractions very well and I Dont understand kg's and g's at all please could you help me I am also not very good at English

Samantha

Perhaps the most striking feature of the journals was their frankness:

> I knew I got the answer right because we had to go through it 25 times This was boring I kept dropping my coin when I was tossing it and Mr H told me off. It wasnt my fault How was I to know I can't toss coins?

Lauren

Sometimes they expressed very clearly the hopelessness of the pupils' predicament. Was I really such an ogre?

> 14.1.87
>
> why didn't you come out — that's why I'n there I was afraid you'd say "you should know that by now!"
>
> This morning we did fractions, well I did anyway! I didn't want to go out to Mrs Rosenfelt for help, so I just sat and tried to work it out myself I couldn't understand.

Nichola

The journals often surprised me. Children felt able to tell me about how they sensed their learning was progressing. Very often they told me things that I really didn't know. Many of the entries demonstrate quite clearly just how crucial self-confidence and self-belief are to learning. Children seem to know this well, but how often do we acknowledge it?

I like maths. When Matths is over I fell – ow no what can I do now. Matths is one of my fuvorite subbjects. That is good.

Michelle

The journals contained plenty of appeals for help and the children became more and more willing to ask questions about what they were doing. I tried to respond either in writing or in a more practical way the next day. I found their genuine response to my comments very rewarding indeed.

Finding the right tone for a response can be quite tricky at first. I found myself using a number of different strategies ranging from full-blown mathematical exposition to the gentle word of encouragement. Often my responses to what the child had written drew a further response from the child herself. In some cases an extensive correspondence developed!

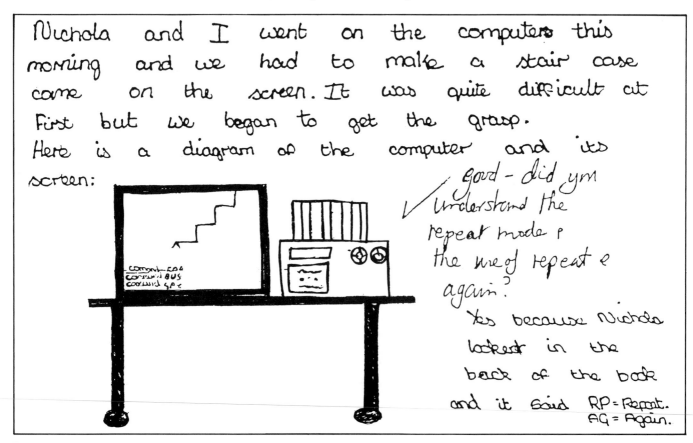

Nichola and I went on the computers this morning and we had to make a stair case come on the screen. It was quite difficult at First but we began to get the grasp.
Here is a diagram of the computer and its screen:

good – did you understand the repeat mode & the use of repeat & again?

Yes because Nichola looked in the back of the book and it said RP = Repeat. AG = Again.

Jemma

Percentages I really understand them now after doing 2 sections of them I'll write one to show you 75% - $\frac{3}{4}$ so 75% of $\overset{12}{\cancel{16}}$ = $\frac{3}{4}$ of 12 = 9 am I write to change a percentage in to a vulgar valgue Fraction you have to find what the percentage is out of a number eg 50% is $\frac{1}{2}$ of 100 : 25% is $\frac{1}{4}$ of 100 75% is $\frac{3}{4}$ of 100; 100% is 1 whole one of 100 that means your've got all the sums write out of a test or none of the apples are f have gone off out of what you bought Miss can you have a percentage out of another number like 12 if? you can, can you expain it to me

You really do seem to understand percentages Sian a great deal more. Per cent means out of a 100 so you are always thinking about the 100 as the whole lot
Think of century - a hundred years.
or cent - there are 100 in a dollar.

Sian

At first some of the children needed the security of simply stating the pages of a book that they had been using or just writing out the problem or investigation. However, from the start some of the children were quite willing to read their journals aloud, even using them to 'teach' the other members of the class, and this acted as a useful catalyst for some who were less confident.

I learned a great deal from what the children wrote. I was able to select points which might need further development or investigation in response to the children's own comments and questions — comments which were far more useful than any 'right' or 'wrong' answer. I began to realise just how anxious many children can be to find the tricks through which they could get their sums correct.

I began to see some of the children in my class in a new light. The genuine communication which took place in the journals helped me to deal with my class in a more sympathetic and understanding way. That alone would have made worthwhile the extra effort needed to read through yet another set of books. In fact, very little effort was needed; reading the journals became an enjoyable task and one which was certainly not a burden because I was not marking in the usual sense.

Some of the journal entries contained keen observations and sparkling insight:

> I have troble with some of the large numbers, but when something is to difficult for you and you get it wrong you learn

Gareth

> I like mostly new maths like a new story. Maths is like a choose your own adventure book, write the wrong answer and fatal death awaits, choose the right answer and a glorious victory to awaits choose to do the hard page or shall I seek help from the wizard (the teacher). So maths is not all bad if look at it my way.

Richard

Perhaps it's really too early to make a proper evaluation of an investigation like this — and there are certainly many ways in which I can further develop this kind of approach in Maths. What is quite clear to me is that I'm getting far more response through the journals than I ever did when I relied purely on talk for feedback, and the journals seem to have promoted a greater willingness to ask questions orally, too. Curiously, a few of the boys in the class are still not writing as freely as I would have hoped, but in the class as a whole there has been an increasing confidence in the way in which many children handle mathematical language and I hope that the fog of mathematical mystique has begun to thin a little. Journal writing will have an important part to play in the Maths curriculum in my classroom in the future.

But perhaps I should leave the last word to Lauren?

> I like writing in my maths journal, because I can scream and shout without making a noise

Margaret Rosenfeld, Croesty Primary School, Pencoed, Bridgend, Mid Glamorgan

Inventing the wheel

Local Studies investigations in the Primary school

The children's machines showed ingenuity and great variety in design and materials. Even more striking, however, were their reflections on the process. The children's familiarity with using journals to help them sort out ideas meant that they could find different routes to learning. They communicated the progress of their ideas and feelings to the teacher, showing both the difficulties . . .

Opportunities for pupils to choose how they write about an area of investigation can lead to unexpected results. Fourth year Juniors in Elise Vear's class at Stourfield School, Bournemouth, spent half a term studying the local river. They looked at the natural history of the area, flood control, the river as a power source, recreational provision, water supply, pollution and farm management. A visit to a water mill was the basis for a Science problem-solving exercise; the pupils were asked to devise their own water wheels from whatever materials they thought would be useful and to prove that they worked. In the classroom they observed a model, developed their own ideas and constructed experiments, recording both the process and the result.

> Our Water Wheels
>
> Monday, 25th. May
> I am thinking how to make it and what out of.
>
> Tuesday, 26th, May
> I am still thinking about it.
>
> Wednesday, 27th, May
> I am thinking about making the wheel we made at school.
>
> Thursday, 28th, May
> I have a different idea. I have some plastic egg cups which are transparent. I also found a round polestryrene thing which I used for the middle. I cut out 8 egg cups but I could only stick on (with blue tap)4. Then I stuck a pen through a hole in the centre I made with the pen. I took my water wheel to the sink and tried it. It would work a bit but the sink wasn't deep enough so I put it under the bath tap. like a charm the wheel whirled round. The tape though peeled off so I used a yellow material tape and it worked well.

. . . and the triumphs.

This careful explanation of experiment and discovery shows how children may be prepared to take great pains with their work. Helen knows that her teacher will be interested in reading her account, so she writes explicitly about the process and particularly about what she sees as successful learning:

'At first I had to think then I came up with two small bottles. I thought I could put three seconds in the bottles so I tried but I did not succeed so I tried again still nothing it did not work because the bottles would not take three seconds so I had to think of something else then I came up with two plastic corks so I tried this I got the two corks and put a milk bottle top between them and put a hole in it then I put sand in I was going to use salt or suger but I thought it might go stale and suger is a bit stickey so I used sand but when I tried The milk bottle top got in the way even though there was a hole in it this happened because the rim of the milk bottle top was being a kind of obstacle for the sand. So then I made another invension. I got an old party popper and where the long bit is I choped that of except for about two centimertas then I got a plastic cork. The bit which was left on the party popper and I put that bit in the cork then I put the sand through the bottom of the popper.

But I found when I put the sand in it went straight through into the cork so I needed a stopper but I didn't want to use my figure so I went round the house to see what I could find and I found a screw so I tried it. It fitted so I tied some cotton and tied it on to the screw the I put the screw through the party popper and put the sand in it took me quit a while to get anogh sand so I put the sand in the party popper and I palled the cotton to list the screw and all the sand went into the cork It was Successful. I wanted to make another Invension so I did I got two sampel bottles from Avon they were empty of course I got enogh sand to time three seconds then I stuck them together with sellotape then I found some wood and stuck them to the bottoms of the bottles It was succes again it was a bit like an eggtimer.'

Journals can give a chance to write about what really matters . . .

> Thursday 3rd June
> used a thing to hold
> wire for the wheel
> and coved it with
> tin foil then cut strips
> of card and cut slits
> in them. Then I made
> card bord squares
> and ~~ebobe~~ stuk them
> in the slits.
> "0" Mrs vear I want
> to tell you about
> a little robin
> in a friends
> work shop it
> workes with him
> and sits on his
> tools and watches
>
> him do his work.
> The first nest she
> made was in a cup
> of tea then a window
> ledge then on top
> of a pile of plastic
> on a shelf ~~that~~ that
> she uses on and
> of all year
> but at the ~~moment~~
> moment she is in
> a ~~umbrell~~ umberella
> with five eggs. when
> we were there he tapped
> the nest and she stuk
> her head out and then
> hopped onto the ~~~~ peice
> of wood
>
> Thank you for the lovely description They are fasanating
> aren't they – much more interesting than the waterwheel!

. . .and an opportunity to explore words and experience:

'Cool mist brushes along your face and leaves a wet mark. Lush green grass gets wet and the cobwebs are visible on the dew.'

'Bronchites has struck me the grey cloud towers over me I shiver as the north wind blows inside.'

'A sheet of glass blocks the sunlight from me. My prison cell stops me getting out as a nightmare starts.'

'The worst is now here. I toss and turn and struggle to breath helplessly in my bed.'

'I start to feel better I see a glimpse of sunlight shining through the grey cloud as the north wind calms down.'

Elise Vear, Stourfield School, Bournemouth, Dorset, with thanks to Helen Carter, Rebecca Dewhurst and Stephen Gardiner

Teachers' comments

'I was interested in the comment about boys being more reluctant to write in their journals. It's made me think about our expectations of what and how boys and girls will write. Do we prevent boys from expressing feelings and discourage girls from more abstract thinking?'

'What would be the children's response to having to write a log in every different subject area? Can we rely upon teachers adopting different strategies, or do collective decisions have to be taken to avoid repetition?'

When reflective writing becomes an everyday opportunity for learning, the experience can be built on by teachers and pupils alike. Recording progress can lead to discussions and negotiations which can be extended to giving parents valuable information. Even in areas which are not traditionally associated with writing, pupils can gain from reflecting on their learning.

Recording children's work

Writing logs in English lessons

I believe we should provide as many opportunities as possible in the classroom for children to value their own writing, reflect on what they have written and appreciate the continuity and progression in their work. One way to achieve this is by using a filing and recording system organised and controlled by the pupils themselves. Every half term I set aside one or two lessons when the children review the work they have done so far in the term and copy or file their best piece. They are encouraged to make their own choice but they may use a partner, trusted friend or teacher to help them make the final decision. If the chosen piece is a long story they photocopy it.

I discuss what constitutes a good piece of work with the children. One useful strategy is to distribute copies of some writing done by a pupil in another school and ask the children in pairs or groups to discuss it and underline three or four 'good bits'. In the class discussion that follows I invariably find that we have all underlined similar lines or phrases. The children are then ready to carry out the same activity with a partner's work. After a few sessions it becomes clear that a successful piece of work does not necessarily mean only a piece of neat writing correctly spelled. The children begin to look for underlying rather than surface qualities and gain confidence in their own judgement.

When they have chosen their work the children are asked to fill in their writing logs. These are kept in their files and serve two purposes. The children are asked to explain why they chose the particular piece of work and are encouraged to reflect on their writing in general. A guide to help them write their logs is available in the classroom.

Writing logs – a guide

Choosing a piece of work

Choose your best piece/s of work done during the last half term.
Consider these points when making your choice:

What were you asked to write about?
How well did you complete the the writing task you were set?
Try not to confuse presentation with content.
In a poem/description look for 'golden lines' to help you find your best piece.
Use your neighbour/response partner/teacher to help if you are not sure but learn to rely on your own judgement too.

Writing in your log

You are free to write what you like but some of these points may help you:

Why did you choose this particular piece?
Why were you asked to write it?
Can you say anything about how you wrote it?
Did you find it easy? Did you write it at home or at school?
Are there any bits you like or dislike particularly?

Write about your work in English generally.

What have you enjoyed writing about?
What other kinds of writing would you like to do?
Would you like to do more or less writing?
What have you learnt so far by practising writing about different things?

I try to stress the importance of the log to the children and explain that when they review their file in two or three years' time they may have forgotten the reasons why they chose a particular piece of work. The log will provide a permanent record of this. Also it can help their teachers to plan work for them if the children record what they find difficult and what they enjoy doing. The files are kept in a ringbinder in the classroom and pupils are encouraged to add to the file and write in their logs at any time.

Obviously the children experience great difficulty at first in discriminating between pieces of work, judging what is good and writing about the reasons for choosing a particular piece. As a recording system, the log is useful and important but the process the children go through is the most valuable part of the exercise. It allows children to evaluate their own work; it acts as a motivator because all pupils want to find something to put in their files. On a number of occasions children have asked me if they can go away and write something new because they are not happy with what's in their book. It gives children confidence. They experience real pleasure when they have a few pieces in their file and can read out examples they are proud of.

The log provides valuable feedback from pupil to teacher on an individual basis. It also provides useful information for parents' evenings and when writing reports. If children change groups or schools the file can give additional information.

Bridget Joslin, Oakfield School, Frome, Somerset

Profiling in P.E.

Secondary pupils record their own progress

Two years ago the school became involved in the Wiltshire Record of Achievement and Profiling Project. Each faculty was given the task of developing a profiling scheme that they felt was appropriate to their needs for introduction to the first year, with a view to expanding year by year up the school until all the year groups were involved. We wanted to integrate the ideas we had developed from our early work into the scheme. We consider summative profiling schemes to be extremely limited in nature compared with the self-assessments through writing which our pupils had made; we wanted to devise a scheme that would become an integral part of the teaching/learning process and not something 'bolted on' at the end.

In particular we discussed:

● For whom was the profile intended? Pupils, parents, teachers, employers? We felt that the emphasis would change as pupils moved up the school, but initially the focus should be on assisting pupils with their learning, and providing some feedback about progress for both teacher and parents.

● What was the purpose of the profile? We were confident that the approach would help to achieve a number of objectives: assessment of achievement; establishing dialogues between all pupils and their teachers; clarifying the aims of P.E.; helping teachers to establish whether what they think they are teaching is being taught; encouraging pupils to take responsibility for their own learning and progress.

● What were we trying to assess? For simplicity we identified five broad areas that reflected the aims of P.E. within our school: fitness for health, physical skills, knowledge and understanding, teamwork, positive attitudes and response in terms of effort and participation.

As a result, we decided that pupils would build up a self-profile during the course of the year by keeping their own P.E. journal/diary.

To help pupils focus on their learning we provided a series of prompt questions related to the objectives of a block of work. These must be to a certain degree open-ended to allow diversity of response. Through question and answer, class discussion and end-of-lesson debriefing, learning is reinforced. This makes profiling an integral part of lessons and allows pupils to review their progress as they go. By the time recording is done, their thoughts will be ordered, keeping writing time to a minimum in what is primarily a practical subject.

Every few weeks the pupils are given ten minutes or so to record their thoughts, progress and achievements in their journals from the prompt questions that have been developed in lessons in the previous few weeks. For simplicity, we have found it works better if the teacher concentrates on one assessment area at a time. The teacher reads and responds after each pupil's entry with a short statement of encouragement or a question about something they have written. As time is at a premium we find that skim-reading and a few words written in the pupil's diary will suffice; this helps to develop the teacher-pupil relationship and shows what they have written to be important.

**KINGSDOWN SCHOOL
PHYSICAL EDUCATION DEPARTMENT
SELF ASSESSMENT PROFILE FOR PERIOD ENDING:**

Name: Tutor Group:

These self assessments have been prepared in consultation with your son's/daughter's Physical Education teacher. The areas of assessment below reflect the main aims of Physical Education at Kingsdown School.

1   FITNESS FOR HEALTH:

2   PHYSICAL SKILLS AND ABILITY:

3   KNOWLEDGE AND UNDERSTANDING (rules and simple tactics):

4   TEAMWORK AND ABILITY TO WORK WITH OTHERS:

5   RESPONSE TO PHYSICAL EDUCATION (effort, participation, involvement):

SPORTS TEAMS AND CLUBS:

ADDITIONAL TEACHER'S COMMENTS (if appropriate):

Signed: (Student)   (Teacher)

Before the P.E. profile document is sent home, the pupils have to reflect on the writing they have done in their journals and select and summarise their views and feelings about their strengths and weaknesses. In negotiation with the teacher these comments are then transferred to the profile document to be sent home at the end of the year. This final process is the most time-consuming, and good organisation and regular entries during the course of the year help keep this to a minimum. Often we feel it appropriate to add our own comment on the profile.

The diversity of pupil response has been enlightening and has led me to question some of my practice and be more self-critical. It has made me aware that there is plenty we can do to improve our teaching. Pupils' and teachers' perceptions often differ as to what they think they have been doing. In my own case it has led to wider use of a variety of teaching styles, with a greater emphasis on pupil input and response in lessons.

The journals should be seen not as testing pupils, but as assisting their learning and understanding. They need to be perceived as useful and important by teachers and pupils alike. A half-hearted approach is not likely to produce favourable results. What is clear is that a dialogue which involves pupils in their own learning can lead to valid and accurate self-assessment.

We are pleased with the benefits of using P.E. journals, but what are the problems? Undoubtedly the biggest problem is loss of practical time in what all of us consider a limited time allowance already. If high activity and participation levels were the only criteria for successful physical education, then this would be a justifiable criticism. We are very aware that we don't want to lose a minute more practical time than is necessary, but feel that the time we spend is of genuine benefit in a complete physical education for all pupils. It helps us as teachers to evaluate the physical education process. There is an increased teacher workload in quickly reading pupils' entries and responding, but it does give teachers much better insights into their pupils and replaces the drudgery of the old system of writing what were quite often meaningless and not particularly accurate reports.

The great strength of working in this way is that it is extremely flexible and can be applied to different subject matter easily. We are now using this method of working in our first and second year classes but adapting our approach as we find some things work better than others. Other Secondary schools in our area are using similar ideas and we hope that in view of their experiences further improvements will be made.

Charles North, Kingsdown School, Swindon, Wiltshire

Teachers' comments

'I had previously used journals most successfully as a way of supporting the teaching of particular novels and poetry; what I wanted to avoid was the "let it all hang out" philosophy of some journals which, as I had seen, could lead to dangerous self-indulgence for both writer and reader. I wanted the subject matter of the logs to be firmly kept in one area of mutual concern: the work. The logs could also serve as a useful base for profiling.'

'In the front of each journal I attach notes explaining to the pupil what they're for and how I'll respond. It's a useful way to explain to parents, too, so they understand what this kind of writing is for.'

'I've always used a journal myself to help me sort out my ideas. I don't know why I didn't think of suggesting it to my classes. I've noticed that they take a bit of time to get used to writing like this, but we share our journals and they soon become an important part of our work.'

Summary

These accounts suggest ways of answering some questions about reading and responding to writing. Moving from the early jottings, notes and plans mentioned in Section 1, these reflective uses of writing add another powerful means for a learner to organise thought, stand back from it and review it. The benefits for learner and teacher seem to be that:

- Journals, learning logs or think books allow learners to work out their own ideas at their own pace; to ask questions which spring from a particular need to know; to speculate about possibilities, clarifying them by the act of writing; to record successes and failures.

- Teachers have the chance to see evidence of learning as it is happening, rather than having to rely on a written account after an activity has taken place, where writing may often reveal what has not been learned.

- The chance for dialogues with individuals can bring surprises. When freed from the constraints of fixed time limits, specific questions about a topic, or concerns about what will happen when a piece of work is marked, learners can show greater confidence and understanding.

- Reflective writing forms a continuing record which both teachers and pupils can use as a basis for discussions about progress; evaluation by both partners in learning becomes an integral part of the process and can be extended to explain and report to parents.

- The teacher's response can be a demonstration of how to tackle ideas, a means of motivation, an explanation of the purpose of any task, and particularly a way of showing children that writing is for reading — by themselves or others.

Using journals, learning logs, think books or diaries has implications for classroom practice, however:

- Introducing a different kind of writing, and perhaps a new way of dealing with children's writing, may need careful explanation — about what the writing is for, who will read it, and how it will be treated.

- The teacher's response may vary according to the way reflective writing is used, and arrangements about responding may require more flexible organisation than marking a set of exercise books.

In developing a range of strategies to respond to children's journal writing and to use the journals to move learning further forward, teachers may need to:

- give guidelines for pupils to respond to their own and other children's writing until they have become familiar and comfortable with reflective writing

- ask questions about entries to prompt ideas

- select particular points for explanation

- notice if boys and girls use their journals differently and use that awareness for sensitive intervention

- arrange times for consultation over journal entries

- allow reflective writing at different times of the day

- write journals themselves

3 The classroom context

Introduction to a range of strategies for learning will not in itself ensure that pupils will be able to choose when to use a particular approach for a given task. To increase confidence, pupils need opportunities to experiment with the expected outcomes. They also need time to try things out, evaluate, change and develop ideas.

How can these opportunities be offered? It may mean moving the furniture, teachers writing alongside pupils or finding different ways of responding to writing. A wider range of reading and writing experiences might be introduced so that pupils can see more clearly the possibilities for writing in different forms. The teacher may need to experiment with new ways in which audiences can be found, or writing displayed or published. Identifying ways in which pupils can be given experience of a variety of writing activities can help in looking afresh at how learning is organised. Since no one strategy will necessarily suit all pupils, creating possibilities for flexibility becomes even more important.

There may be a shift in the teacher's role when pupils are encouraged to take on more responsibility for their own learning. What are the implications for planning and organisation? When learning tasks are seen as long-term activities which require response to writing at different stages, there is a greater need for classroom management which will encourage and support collaboration and the sharing of ideas at certain times. Sometimes this can be disconcerting but it is certainly challenging. Sensitive guidance, response and intervention are even more necessary and ingenuity is needed in developing methods of consultation which can form part of everyday classroom organisation. Even if pupils use each other as partners in learning, the teacher's role is fundamental in making sure that collaboration is fruitful and positive.

The accounts in this section outline ways in which teachers have increased the variety of their pupils' writing experiences. They focus particularly on different aspects of organisation in the classroom. Collaborative work, gathering material to inform others, publishing writing and encouraging more reflective uses of writing all require careful planning on the teacher's part. Descriptions of both the successes and the constraints offer suggestions for writing opportunities which allow more flexible approaches to learning.

They're only six years old

Collaborative activities with Infants

After a 'writers in school' residential course I came back to school bursting with ideas. I threw myself in at the deep end with my top Infants and started off some collaborative work.

We had very recently been given as a present three baby male gerbils. The children were delighted and immediately wanted hands-on experience. Our very first problem was to choose names. Suggestions were written on the white board. How would we decide? The children thought carefully and came up with an elimination points system which worked admirably. The gerbils were thus named Richy, Rocky and Ripple.

We realised that if we were to care for the gerbils properly there were problems to

When children have some responsibility for their own learning they can surprise us with their capabilities. Jenni Tribello and Jean Lediard, with widely differing age groups, found that chances to collaborate meant that their classes became more actively involved in the planning and organisation of their own work.

be solved, questions to ask ourselves and rules to be written. These problems were real and relevant and therefore the work was necessary.

We sat and had a long discussion about how we needed to organise a good lifestyle for the creatures and ourselves. We came up with:

1 A set of rules for handling gerbils

2 Scientific facts — what sort of creatures they were, where they come from, eating, nesting, mating habits

3 Information leaflets for weekends — for mums and dads

4 Profiles — so we could tell them apart

5 An information poster

6 New designs for the cage — necessities and extras

7 A comic — light-hearted jokes, cartoons and stories to overcome any fears

8 A Bill of Rights — what gerbils could hope to expect of life and the respect they would hope to receive

Everyone agreed these were necessary areas. Then came what I thought would be the difficult task of grouping the children for writing. It turned out to be easy. We had talked earlier about what skills were necessary to complete a piece of work: a secretary, a good speller, a brainstormer, an artist and a leader. The idea of working collaboratively certainly excited the children and when choosing time came they chose sensibly and wisely, not necessarily choosing best friends. I knew I couldn't have chosen better myself.

By now we had been discussing for quite some time, and a bright spark piped up with *'When can we get on with our work?'* I felt they'd got the message. We sorted out rough paper areas, who would sit next to the gerbils first, who needed to go and find research material and the general working areas. I kept reminding myself that they were only six years old.

They learned a lot about each other that first week. I learned a lot too. If I'm honest, the less confident children at times seemed lost but this was only to be expected. However, I believe that through constant short discussion times we were able to overcome most difficulties.

The finished work was proof in itself, if I needed proof. It was attractive and informative, and the children were pleased with themselves. For me it once again proved that you should never underestimate children, whatever their age. They had responded to this new working experience in such a positive way that I knew there would never be any going back.

We are now two months on and further committed to collaborative work. We are writing books in pairs for younger children. We have Maths response partners and partners for practically everything. The children talk over their work with each other and help each other, and consequently the quality of work has improved. Proof indeed.

Jenni Tribello, Four Lanes Primary School, Basingstoke, Hampshire

The Healthy Eating campaign

Secondary pupils write information material

My third year English class at Pencoed Comprehensive needed to have an experience of writing for an audience other than themselves or me. I thought it would be helpful to them if they tackled a topic which they knew about and which would require a wide variety of writing activities. Earlier in the term they had directed some written work at one other third year class. This time we decided to produce a Healthy Eating campaign with all the third year pupils as the target audience.

It was important that their publications should be of a suitable standard for the intended audience and particularly important to me that the work should be collaborative. I explained these aims to the class, asking them to negotiate the membership and organisation of the groups themselves. We talked about making notes while researching the topic and how these could be used as a basis for the group discussion. We also discussed possible forms of outcome.

After picking up a few useful nutrition leaflets from a supermarket, I wrote to the company who very helpfully sent me thirty copies of each. The class divided into groups of four and read through all the leaflets. One person in each group took responsibility for a specific leaflet and summarised the main points. These summaries were then compared across groups to make sure that the most relevant facts had been included. This was one of the most difficult parts to organise. The class then discussed how best to communicate the information to other third year pupils. They decided that they wanted to make posters and booklets and present an assembly about healthy eating. Then came the really tricky part — how to organise the whole activity.

All the pupils wanted to start with a survey of the eating habits and views on nutrition of the other third years. Each group worked out questions that they thought would give them useful information, and then one of the groups took responsibility for the overall process and presentation of the findings as a wall chart. Outcomes which the group planned were:

- a pamphlet entitled 'Healthy Eating' incorporating interviews with canteen staff and teachers about school dinners

- posters

- a news-sheet called 'Health Journal' giving facts about healthy food

- taped speeches for assembly

- a booklet of recipes and information for pupils who liked cooking

The groups worked enthusiastically and I was pleased to see how much the pupils learned in three to four weeks by being actively involved in planning and organising their own work both during their English lessons and at home. I could not have taught them during a whole term what they learned during that period about:

- framing survey questions so that the responses could be collated easily

- analysing results

- presenting results in a variety of appropriate forms

- conducting interviews; adapting prepared questions in the light of answers

- making eye-catching designs

- preparing, editing and presenting condensed information in booklet form

- writing concise speeches and delivering them in an entertaining way

The work generated a great deal of discussion about their joint enterprise and the use of technical and everyday language needed to get the messages across. The pupils helped each other and shared ideas. They were supported in their efforts by their form teacher, a Biology specialist, who showed interest in displaying the finished work.

Although the pupils were satisfied that they had gained from the work and were pleased to see their final products as posters and booklets, there were some difficulties and sticking points. Some of the problems were technical: for example, although groups spent time after school working on their tape recordings for the assembly these were unsuccessful and the children eventually had to make their presentations 'live'. This, too, was difficult because the assembly was held in the dining hall where there was a lot of background noise, so that much of what they had to say couldn't be heard. As a class we were satisfied with both the process and the finished products, but the booklets didn't get much response from the target group of other third year classes. This may have been because the standard of handwritten presentation didn't look professional enough. Perhaps, more importantly, the intended audience wasn't ready for such a campaign.

I know that I feel more dissatisfied about this than the pupils do since they clearly enjoyed the activities and gained much useful experience of writing for different purposes. When I plan for another class to do a similar campaign I shall want to think more carefully about how to capture the audience's interest, and how to gain more support and interest from colleagues who teach other subjects. One way to do this may be to ask what information resources would be useful in other curriculum areas, and to let a class choose topics as commissioned researchers and writers. My other main concern is to do with final presentation, and how to deal with typing and duplication without the writers having to wait too long for their publications to see the light of day. How many times can you suggest that writers redraft their work if it's going to be a handwritten final product? Am I more concerned about presentation than the pupils are, and if so, who is right? These are some of the questions I shall try to deal with when I tackle something like this again.

Jean Lediard, Pencoed Comprehensive School, Bridgend, Mid Glamorgan

Teachers' comments

'Writing for an audience other than the teacher is vital for all writers, but especially perhaps for the third year pupils who may well need to see a point to their efforts and feel they are sharing ideas and being valued.'

'I found the ideas worked well in practice. The children produced a book to communicate with another school. They collaborated in writing the material for the book and the introduction. Collaboration worked well with mixed ability groups. All the children, at all levels, had something to offer and all felt valued. They also used partners for proof-reading and drafting their stories. The children produced a piece of work that was well constructed, beautifully presented and full of spontaneity.'

'I would like to explore collaborative work much further across the curriculum. We have been doing this to a certain extent in Maths and now we have experienced some success we would like to do more in Topic and Science work.'

'Concern has been expressed about the attitude of some parents to children working on joint projects rather than individual assignments. It was felt that parents needed to be kept informed of the benefits through open days, curriculum evenings and invitations to participate.'

Living History

Interviews by seven-year-olds

With some trepidation I chose to use an interview as a stimulus for my class of thirty-two seven-year-olds. I had never used this method before and I felt my children were perhaps too young to benefit from it.

I was fortunate to have a ready-made interviewee in the shape of my aunt who is ninety years old. Although infirm of limb she is very alert mentally, and she readily agreed to help me.

It was Harvest Festival time at school, and we had been talking about why we bring our gifts and what happens to them after the service. We discussed what it would mean to an elderly person to receive a parcel from us. I invited my aunt to come along to the service. The children did not have an opportunity to talk to her but it was a chance to sow the seed ready for her visit the following week.

I gave the children a little background information about my aunt, Mrs Parton. She was born at the end of the last century during the reign of Queen Victoria, and has lived all her life in Rochdale. The children and I discussed the questions we could ask her about what it was like to be a child in Rochdale eighty years ago. I wrote out the questions and duplicated them so that each child could have a copy.

The children were very excited when the time came for Mrs Parton's visit. They asked their questions clearly and sensibly and my aunt did very well in answering them, even telling us more than we had asked for in many cases. I taped the interview and the children thoroughly enjoyed using the microphone. The

In seeking to stimulate their pupils' learning and introduce more variety into the writing curriculum in their classrooms, teachers have found that experiences outside the classroom can provide inspiration. At a time when resources are difficult to come by, it's easy to forget the human resources within the classroom and the community which can add zest to learning and help pupils gain a greater understanding of the world around them.

following day we filled in the questionnaire using the answers Mrs Parton had given us, and then the children wrote an account of the visit.

I made a classroom display of the children's work along with books and photographs which my aunt had lent to us. We then invited her back to see our efforts, listen to the recording of the interview and hear the children read their writing. Even the less fluent readers were keen to read their stories themselves. This was an enjoyable time for everyone and the children gained a lot from the experience.

Our contact with Mrs Parton did not end there. We wrote to invite her to school for a small party to celebrate her ninetieth birthday. We made biscuits to have with our cups of tea and presented her with some flowers and the cards we had made for her. This was an exciting time for the children, especially when Mrs Parton gave each of them some sweets to take home. I am planning to do some work this term about life in Edwardian times for which we will be able to consult her again for her recollections. I intend to foster the friendship throughout the rest of this school year because I feel it has been a very worthwhile project for all concerned. My initial hesitancy about this work proved to be unfounded and I was pleasantly surprised and very pleased with the results.

Bernice Miller, Brimrod County Primary School, Rochdale

But is it really Geography?

Secondary pupils use writing to explore ideas

I have always considered myself something of a traditionalist as far as my Geography teaching is concerned. The writing that I normally expect from my pupils has been predictable in its nature, and its content has been heavily geared towards geographical facts.

On joining my school Writing Project group in September 1986 I found myself faced with the question, *'What kinds of writing do you expect from your pupils?'* My answer was very clear — all the written work would be very much subject-orientated with little scope for pupils' own ideas or individualistic writing. I decided to experiment which some aspects of teaching the subject.

Before I put my new ideas into operation, I was still somewhat sceptical as to the outcome. Would the introduction of new methods of recording the subject mean sacrificing geographical information? *'Is it really Geography?'* I kept thinking.

I began by asking a class of first year pupils to describe four contrasting photographs.

Ruth wrote:

'Photograph A is about a town or city. It shows lots of factories and high rise buildings which might be flats or offices. This picture makes me think of dirt and smoke because of factory fumes and smoke from the chimneys and fumes from cars. These buildings suggest that lots of people live in the city. I wouldn't like living there because I wouldn't like breathing in that air.'

Carys wrote:

'This is a photograph of a desert area — very hot and dry. Sand dunes are practically all that can be seen except for a few people travelling on camels. People do live here, in large tribes near oases. The camels are used because they can travel for several days without water and move without food. They have adapted to the heat. It may be the Sahara.'

I found the geographical content surprisingly accurate, and the pupils' writing conveyed many other ideas as well, such as the problems of pollution and their likes and dislikes about living in a particular environment. I was also surprised by their readiness to hypothesise and predict.

Spurred on by this initial success I set a fifth year group a role-play exercise relating to their coursework on the coal industry. I divided the class into groups. Some represented the NCB management, and others represented the NUM or village community groups. Each group was asked to put forward in writing its arguments for or against pit closures. The pupils were provided with various stimulus and reference materials, such as a BBC programme entitled 'The future of coal', assorted leaflets on the coal-mining industry in South Wales and an article from the *South Wales Echo*, 'When hope died at the pit left in the cold', about the effects of the closure of Penrikyber Colliery.

I felt that the results were very rewarding both for the pupils and for myself. The assignment revealed sophisticated levels of writing competence well beyond my own expectations, and showed that they had understood the different points of view.

Rosalyn wrote, on behalf of management:

'The geological factors involving this colliery must also be taken into account. Here the coal is now proving very costly to mine because of its position. The present seam has relatively little coal left and it has been decided to close the colliery, within the next two years at most. Surveys have shown us that new seams are either too far away or too deep to be mined from this colliery. Apart from this, the lower parts of the seam are being adversely affected by flooding and may have weakened the surrounding areas of rock. The proposed "superpit" at Margam will provide jobs for those not accepting voluntary redundancy and will continue supporting the industry well into the next century, as will many other pits in the area.'

Interestingly, Joanna and Yvette chose to write rather differently in defence of a mining village:

'Our community would be split up if the colliery closed. There is still coal in the mines but it is far away from the shaft so the NCB want to close them. Even if the pits are uneconomical there are still workable reserves left. The NCB want to spend money on Selby but if they updated the Welsh pits, there is still a lot of coal left in them.'

The conclusion that I've drawn from all this is that many aspects of Geography do lend themselves to a written approach rather different from the one that has traditionally been used, without losing the factual geographical content. Given the right sort of stimulus and opportunity, it can be seen that pupils of all ages and abilities can produce a variety of surprising and rewarding written work. And, yes, it *is* still Geography!

Edryd Evans, Lewis Girls' Comprehensive School, Ystryd Mynach, Mid Glamorgan

Teachers' comments

'Interviewing is a tricky business, particularly for young children. They may think that they have to write down everything the person says, or they don't hear answers because they're busy thinking up the next question. I found the suggestions here helpful; discussing questions and then having a general format allows the teacher to show the difference between "closed" and "open" questions, and the use of the tape for back-up means that they have "captured" important information.'

'I feel that the "best" written work at the moment still comes from the "concrete" — that is, the children writing about something they have examined, experienced or heard, or something that simply interests them.'

'It was interesting to see Geography students using their own community experience. We're in a very different area and much emphasis is given to world studies. As I read this article it struck me that the girls were very adept at voicing the concerns of economic managers — mostly men in the western world — and that I'd like to try with my mixed classes encouraging this kind of writing from the point of view of women who are the major economic providers in other parts of the world.'

Failing doesn't always matter

A CDT project with fourth year Juniors

Writing often accompanies practical activities, but is sometimes seen simply as a record of what has been done. The last three accounts in this section show how teachers have linked the practical applications of CDT, Science and French with a great variety of writing.

I began the project by asking the children to suppose that they were on a solo flight to a particular country, and that they had crashed on the way. Using atlases, they chose both the country of their destination and the one in which they crashed. To find out more about their chosen countries they did research in the reference library and wrote to the relevant embassy asking for more information, particularly about the more remote areas. They took great care over these letters and most of the embassies responded well, some even writing to the children personally and encouraging them in their work.

Their next writing task was to complete a newspaper article reporting on the fact that they were missing, giving their name, details of the flight and a potted autobiography. The children used the computer program 'Front Page' to write another article reporting that a search had been initiated but that it had been unsuccessful. This work showed that the children were able to write clearly in the third person, many of them taking a leap in imagination by writing hypothetically about themselves.

Meanwhile, the children had started writing a journal of their adventures in books which they had made at the beginning of term. These were written in the first person and involved recounting the facts in the first newspaper report from a different viewpoint, explaining why they had crashed, how they had escaped, and what tools and equipment they had rescued.

As they could expect to be stranded for quite a while, the children each planned and built a model shelter such as they might have made for themselves after crashing their aeroplane. Using only natural materials which they collected and brought into school themselves, and string, plasticine and glue instead of nails, screws or rope, they worked collaboratively with much consultation and discussion. They devised tests to find out how stormproof their shelters were and made notes as they went along. Using these notes, they wrote again in their journals, describing the building of the shelters and the storm which followed.

> 5th September
>
> The weather hasn't been lovely since I crashed it hasn't rained at all I've decided to build a shelter while the weather is nice so that I will be prepared What I have done ; I've got 4 big branches and tied them like this ⋈ ⋈ and then put a big branch along the top of the V shape, then I layed other branches over the base and put leaves on them I have n't finished yet but I will soon when I've finished I would like it to look like this

Continuing the Design Technology theme, I invited the children to imagine that they had found some clay near their shelter and with clay from school they each made a small oil lamp. When they were dry, these were packed into a small kiln which the children built in the school playground. This first kiln was a complete failure: the following morning, the children discovered that the fire had quickly died and none of the lamps had been fired. Between us we devised a second design and the lamps were fired successfully this time.

The children were very excited by this activity and their written work flowed naturally from it. They were able to describe clearly and in great detail the processes used in making the lamps and kilns but, more interestingly, they were able to use their imaginations to adapt these concrete ideas for use in their journals. They hadn't been daunted by having to build a second kiln; they were learning to evaluate and assess their own work and to accept and overcome failure.

My lamp

Today I ~~made~~ decided to look around.
I waded through the river ~~it~~ was~~n't~~
all that deep and whin I got to the
other side I found ~~o~~ some clay.
I took as much as I could hold and
~~took off my jumper and~~ waded
back to the other side I then did ~~the~~
this: First I got a round ~~ball shape~~
lump of clay then I took a small
peice out of it and made it into
a sausage shape. Then I made the
round ~~bit~~ Shape into a diamond
shape like this
I put my thumbs ⬡ into the lamp
and dug it out. ⬠ then
got some clay and a ~~little~~ little
bit of water from the stream and I
mixed the clay and ~~watt~~ water
together. ~~then~~ I got the Sausage
shape and cut a mark with my
screwdriver like this ▦
then I did the same with the ~~S~~ lamp

▦ ~~then~~ I got the slip
which is Clay and water ✱
stuck the sausage shape on
the lamp.   ✱ mixed together

Alongside this work the children were also using the *Science Horizons* topic 'Flying starts here'. One of the activities had been for the children to read and follow a set of simple instructions for making paper aeroplanes. After making and testing the planes for distance of flight, the children attempted to write instructions of their own. They found this quite difficult at first but decided on a way of testing the quality of their instructions using younger children. The seven- and eight-year-olds listened to the instructions and tried to carry them out. If there were any difficulties the fourth year child gave further directions which were recorded by a friend who had been chosen as secretary. Eventually, after discussion, a satisfactory set of instructions was produced and the first year children went away happy with their paper planes.

1. First get a piece of paper 28 by 22.
2. Fold in half. lengh-ways
3. Fold top corners into middle
4. Fold the triangular edges into the middle
5 Fold in half
6 Fold point in
7 make wings
8 Fold tip of wing up
9 Make flaps
10 Selotape fusalage.

to touch the middle fold

Fold wings down.
so it stands up.
cut flaps one on each wing at the end.
Selotape wing and tape undern
Cut the plane in the middle

In their journals the children finally wrote about their escape and return to civilisation.

The children's experiences have made me more aware of their untapped potential, their inventiveness, their willingness to learn from one another, and the variety of writing they are able to use.

Sue Phillips, Burnham Copse Junior School, Basingstoke, Hampshire

Experiments with writing

Science in the Primary school

Traditionally, children have been asked to write in a particular way in Science — impersonally and to a fairly rigid format. However, that way of doing things may well inhibit children's development both as scientists and as writers.

It seems that different kinds of writing may serve different purposes for learning in Science. Obviously, it's important that we should be able to use the most appropriate form for the purpose. If children are going to be able to make the necessary decisions about format — about how to record, reflect on and present their work — then we need to provide them with as wide a choice as possible of the different strategies that are available.

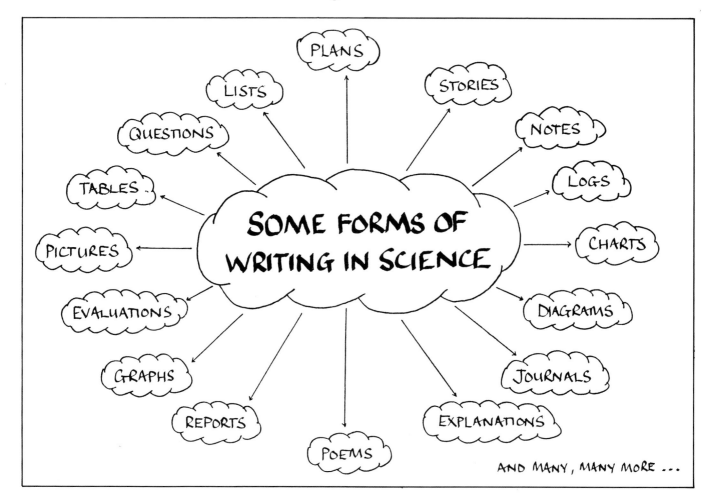

The following examples demonstrate some of the many forms that may be used. The first ones are taken from work done by a class of nine- and ten-year-olds at Twyn-y-rodin Junior School who were investigating the subject of 'Changes'. Each small group of children published their findings, which they offered in various forms, in a group book. The work included:

Lists:

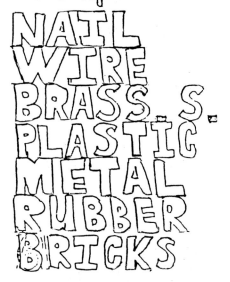

CAN

easily be returned to what it was before.   Reversible

NAIL
WIRE
BRASS. S.
PLASTIC
METAL
RUBBER
BRICKS

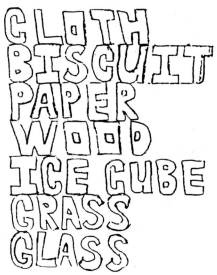

CANNOT

easily be returned to what it was like before.   Irreversible

CLOTH
BISCUIT
PAPER
WOOD
ICE CUBE
GRASS
GLASS

Stories:

In the summer I always go on my bike In the winter I put it in the shed because the nights are going darker then in the spring out it comes again. One winter my mother said Put that bike in the shed for winter. So I took It up to the shed.

That winter must have been the worst It snowed and hail, rain, everything mixed in. All the time I longed to go on my bike and ride to the park and back

It seemed to be so long. Summer came When I went to get my bike it was full of rust

Quickly I went to Halfords to get rust remover Then a soft cloth mit and a few days later it was finished. As I rode it out it shone as if to say "Thankyou for cleaning me".

Poems:

Slipping slithering
Through my fingers,
Water to us
Like an elusive nothing,
An invisible substance
Sliding away.
But to the scientist
A cluster of molecules
Made up of atoms –
Two of hydrogen
And one of oxygen.
A fascinating liquid
That quenches thirst
A silver substance
That makes leaves shine
And grasses smile
In a summers day,
Important for the survival
Of all mankind –
Friend and foe,
But to the scientist
Just H2O.

. . . even reports like these from six-year-olds:

We made a parrot
with card but it
wouldont balanee.
It kept falling oyer on
Its head we put
Plastercine on its toil
to makeit balance

When we balanced
the ruler it balanced
as far as · 14 cm on its
own 17 cm with 1 rubber
18 cm with 2 rubbers
19 cm With 3 rubbers
The more rubbers we used
the bigger piece of ruler
balanced over the table

We often ask children to write reports or accounts of what they have done in their Science investigations even if our ideas about the purpose of those reports aren't always very clear, with consequent confusion in the children's writing. However, the purpose may become much clearer if the work is published for a real audience, inside or outside the classroom.

Publication can mean many things in a classroom context:

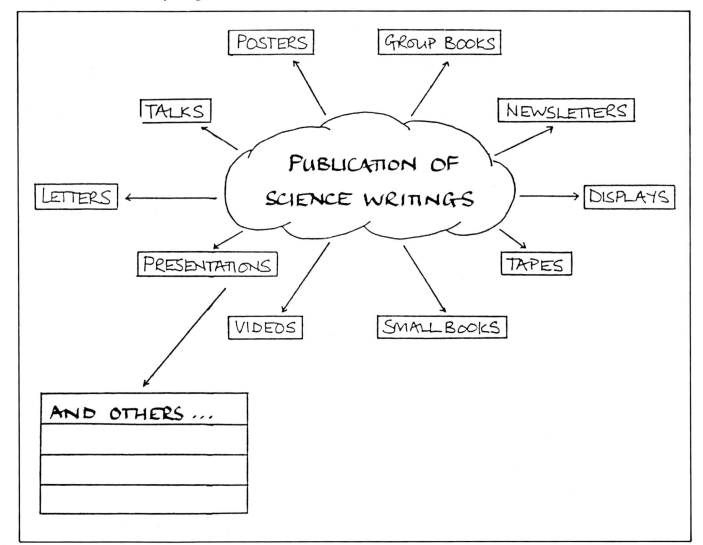

As well as giving the writing a clear purpose, the publication of children's work offers opportunities to share ideas and experiences with others, making the classroom and the school a real community of active scientists!

Yvonne Bacchetta, Primary Science Consultant, Mid Glamorgan
and Richard Landy, Mid Glamorgan Writing Project Co-ordinator

Writing for other audiences in French

Middle school activities

Whilst attending a short English course after school I realised that some superb work was being done in various local English departments on the theme of writing for a purpose. At the time I was teaching English to first years at St Osmund's Middle School, Dorchester, and was able tentatively to put a few of the ideas and suggestions into practice in my French lessons, too.

The obvious beginning was to link classroom displays to the current French coursework. The third year class has recently started French, and this was a method of reinforcing what they had learned in a constructive and enjoyable way. The tasks included label-writing on pre-cut card, cutting out images from bright sugar paper, making A4-size drawings and writing sentences to go with them, collating finished work and positioning it on the wall. Each child chose to do what (s)he felt capable of doing. A classroom display of this sort usually occupied one forty-five minute session.

The third years also made simple games which reinforced grammar points or new vocabulary. The games proved to be less easy to make — a long-winded process which was not easy to co-ordinate in a large class. Games, however, last longer than a wall display and can be used by many pupils as revision work.

With the fourth year class who would be leaving the school at the end of the year, I decided to build on their earlier experience of writing short story books in their English lessons. The children were given a free choice as to the end result for their books but they had to: plan everything in rough as on a film storyboard; use quarter, half or full size A4 for photocopying ease; and have a clear idea of the educational value for other children. The time spent on this project amounted to five forty-five minute sessions plus some homework time.

My aim was that the children should develop their language while making books that others would enjoy reading. They produced material that introduced one particular theme such as 'colours', 'clothes', 'numbers', 'months' and 'seasons'. In this way they were naturally providing the material we require in our school French library. They produced readers which were easy without being too babyish in presentation, knowing instinctively what would appeal to other children.

As leavers the class felt a real purpose for writing the French books. Rather than being for their own use, the books were to help others in the following year enjoy what they had learned in their French lessons. They had to plan their work sensibly and accurately before attempting the end product. In making decisions about the size of the book, the use of pictures, the size of the lettering etc., the children developed many of the skills we teach across the curriculum. They also learned to collaborate closely with others. Equally important was the sense of achievement that groups or individuals felt when they finally signed their names on the books and then passed them around for their friends to read.

Following the success of both these class activities I now have ideas for further work for others to read, use and enjoy.

For younger children:

- making full size road signs, street signs, menus, shop fronts for directions and drama work

- crossword competition

- French newsletter

- letters to tourist offices, companies

- 3D town plan with toy vehicles, card buildings

For older children:

- French limericks, poems, short stories produced for others in book or magazine form

- advertisements, information posters

- radio slots with music in between, disc jockey's commentary, weather and road reports

- fashion show with compères describing clothes, music, prices

Sue Cottam, St Osmund's Middle School, Dorchester, Dorset

Other ideas for extending the audiences for children's writing can be found in the final article 'Write across the curriculum'.

Teachers' comments

'The CDT advisory teacher and I have been team-teaching for a while and have found an enormous variety of writing and interesting stimulus that we could try. We'd been working on instructions and "interest guides" for younger pupils, but hadn't thought of bringing in more imaginative work.'

'I think the child's poem in the Science section is a perfect example of how a scientific write-up needn't be like the old formula. I've used it to show my pupils as a way they might try to write.'

'I found the French activities a real "shot in the arm". I've already tried out writing in French for the younger children and found we all enjoyed it. It's often difficult to find interesting writing to consolidate their learning which isn't just repetitive exercises.'

'We got really carried away with the Fashion Show idea. After all, we use French magazines as background material with the older pupils and this was a good chance to look at French culture as well as a way of encouraging oral work in a real way. The pupils got so involved in the ideas that they decided that both boys and girls should be "models".'

'One of the things that's struck me about group work in Science is how much more chance I get to watch what's going on. It's been an eye-opener. Even with very little children the tendency is for boys to do the experiments and girls to watch or write down the results. It's worrying and I'm not sure how best to deal with it. I think it's best not to make a fuss, but to organise activities so that everyone has to do a bit of everything. Once they get used to it at five and six they seem to mix better later on.'

> ## For discussion
>
> Colleagues might like to use the diagram 'Some forms of writing in Science' to develop more ideas or to look at possible forms of writing in other areas of the curriculum.

Summary

This section has outlined not only a broad range of writing opportunities but also some issues of classroom management which need attention when trying to offer a greater variety of writing experiences. Establishing a classroom environment which encourages active involvement by pupils, elements of choice and negotiation and different uses of writing is bound to present some problems and challenges. The descriptions of classroom activities offer practical ways of tackling the constraints.

The accounts suggest a shift from teaching just the content of a particular curriculum area towards establishing ways of working which will make it easier for learners to see the relevance and importance of what is to be learned. Underlying all the accounts are certain assumptions about children and learning:

- Even very young children have experience which can be drawn upon to make learning more effective.

- Talking and exchanging ideas with each other and the teacher, alongside writing, is an important and valuable way to consolidate learning.

- Children need to be given help in developing new strategies for group work, research or recording, so that they will gain confidence in working more independently.

- Finding opportunities for children to practise new techniques; to understand what they can do with writing; to see the relevance of learning, can result in far greater achievement than the teacher may have thought possible.

- When pupils have a chance to take an active part in their learning; to write for known readers; to publish their writing or see the relevance of classroom work to life outside school, their grasp of new ideas is significantly improved.

- Choice of how to go about a writing task can give children a chance to demonstrate potential which may lie undetected when carrying out routine written assignments.

It is sometimes difficult to view one's own teaching objectively, and the accounts in this section do not always make explicit the careful interventions which the teachers made so that their pupils would be challenged and stimulated to greater achievement in writing and learning. A more open approach to organising classrooms for learning may include:

- making decisions and judgements in the light of experience about how groupings may best be organised

- planning how to introduce and demonstrate new ways of working

- discussing the purposes and aims of learning activities with pupils
- offering signposts and structures within which pupils can learn to succeed or fail with confidence; to respond to their own and others' work
- suggesting or finding particular audiences for writing
- providing materials other than textbooks and exercise books
- offering models or examples of different forms of writing
- finding ways of publishing or presenting pupils' work for others
- advising on layout and presentation as well as helping to edit and revise writing
- explaining criteria for assessing writing and providing ways for pupils to evaluate their own work
- taking decisions about when to intervene and when to stand back

4 Collaborating with colleagues

The previous three sections have looked at the learner organising knowledge through writing; evaluating ideas through dialogues with the teacher and other pupils; and practising new strategies for learning in the environment of a classroom which can support and extend these capabilities. This section moves beyond the individual classroom or subject area to explore ways in which teachers working together can make further connections in learning. Connections between previously separated areas of knowledge can bring significant shifts in understanding including considerations about writing which cross classroom or subject boundaries. It implies the need for teachers to work together to plan joint approaches to writing and learning.

There are, however, obstacles and constraints to such joint activities and it would be foolish to ignore them. These might be related to the organisation of the curriculum where subjects are perhaps arranged discretely into independent programmes of work, or larger organisational difficulties created because teachers work in separate departments which may have differing perceptions and priorities about learning. These organisational factors mean that often there is little opportunity for colleagues to co-operate in planning or discussing learning activities. Even where those curricular and institutional constraints aren't present, time is a major factor. Effective collaboration needs time to talk, to air common problems, to sort out difficulties and to begin to develop a common approach. For all sorts of reasons, collaborating with colleagues isn't easy.

Given the constraints, how can teachers reach common understanding about learning? In this section, teachers describe both the problems and the opportunities which joint ventures have offered. In each account they acknowledge the constraints which they experienced.

A plague on all our syllabuses

A joint venture between Biology, English and History departments

In the mournful atmosphere of a post-full-inspection depression, our school working group met to talk about ways of looking at how the writing curriculum operated in our different subject areas. We all felt that we weren't really making anything like enough use of the possibilities that cross-curricular approaches to learning might offer, and we began to think of ways in which we might make some practical links. In conversation it emerged that the pupils in the first year would all, at some point, be looking at the subject of 'plagues' in both History and Biology. What an opportunity! The English department offered to become involved and we agreed to plan a programme of work together which would try to exploit the opportunities for writing and learning in each department.

We found very quickly that in the context of a typical comprehensive school this is sometimes easier said than done. Perhaps the major problem was rooted in the origins of our investigation; we had seized on a topic which at times meant that we became much more bogged down in syllabus considerations than perhaps was necessary. We spent time trying to reconcile and compromise our differences and eventually agreed on an action plan involving a first year class which we all taught.

One of the most important things we found was that many of the learning

Primary school teachers have known the benefits of working through a topic or theme in a cross-curricular way for a long time. However, it is not an approach which is commonly adopted in Secondary schools. In the following accounts, teachers from two comprehensive schools describe how they attempted to break down some difficult barriers in order to offer their pupils a more varied diet of writing.

resources to which we had access served all sorts of purposes in different subject areas. For example, a play called *Ring o' roses*, which was used in Biology to introduce the Great Plague, formed the basis of much of the subsequent work in English — the children remaining in and extending their roles. In fact, this kind of cross-referencing occurred much more readily in the children's learning than in our planning; children in their History lessons quite frequently passed on information which they had come across in Biology and were quick to correct the English teacher when he made a mistake about dates or symptoms. We found that the collaborative approach we had adopted appeared to raise the interest level among the pupils. One commented later:

'I enjoyed doing them all at the same time because you can use the knowledge from one lesson to help you put down something different in another.'

The extended use of roles and the opportunity to research across the boundaries of the curriculum certainly seemed to create a greater sense of purpose in the pupils' writing, and they responded very positively to the greater variety of possible formats which they were offered. Some tasks were undertaken by all the pupils in 1D, some by groups of pupils and some individually, including:

- historical newspapers which contained a series of headlines and news items describing the arrival of the plague, its effects on the people and the country and its departure

- diaries describing what happened to people when the plague hit their village. These diaries were strongly empathetic and demonstrated clearly a deep level of engagement in the work

- experiments with data-handling using information about the Great Plague

- posters: warnings to the inhabitants of the village, advertisements for lucky charms and miracle cures and 'wayside pulpit' style messages; charts illustrating the spread of the disease and the number of deaths

- notes for their own presentations (mostly in role) to the rest of the class. These included an address by the town crier, a hell fire sermon by the priest, a quack's sales patter, the doctor's medical advice and interviews with the inhabitants

- a very successful and beautifully presented board game which is in itself a valuable teaching resource, based on the Plague and complete with chance cards and charms

- maps and other display materials to help set the scene in the village

Some older pupils helped 1D to make a short video programme, complete with commentary, based on the class presentations they had done. Although there were the usual infuriating technical difficulties and we really needed much more time, this mode of publishing the work was very much appreciated.

Eventually 1D put their work in the Plague project together as an exhibition to entertain visiting pupils from the local Primary schools.

The pupils certainly learned a lot and there is plenty of evidence to show that because of the connections which they were able to make across the curriculum, the learning was effective, more purposeful and more fun. There was genuine excitement at the idea of being involved in a project which the pupils clearly perceived as being original and very much their own.

We learned a lot, too, about how to make these kinds of links more effective. We've already mentioned the difficulties caused by choosing a topic that we'd all tackled separately before. The tendency to do what we'd done in the way that we'd done it was always there. In a sense, we needed to start with a completely blank sheet of paper so that past practice wouldn't dominate our planning. More time was needed — both for the detailed planning and for the project work itself. Inevitably, most of the writing was left to English lessons (more time being allocated for those) and we might have done better to see ourselves more as a team of teachers, all concerned with language development as a primary aim.

Perhaps our choice of topic was too narrow. A broader topic might well have extended the cross-curricular nature of the pupils' investigations further, particularly if the topic were based on a concept rather than facts. In short, we weren't really ambitious enough. But we're certainly keen to try again. The pupils' own enthusiasm for this way of working makes sure of that:

'I felt kind of happy when we first started but when I read on I thought for a minute to think what it was like for those people, not knowing what hit them. When we wrote the diary about the plague it sounded as if you were really there in that village. Now the project is over my feelings are still with the plague.'

Christine Ashman, Richard Landy, Jean Lediard, Mike Mcloughney, Julie Phillips and Mike Tibbott
Pencoed Comprehensive School, Bridgend, Mid Glamorgan

Writing on the Home Front

English, History, R.E. and Home Economics join up

During our first year in the Writing Project we'd all undertaken different investigations into ways of extending the kinds of writing opportunities we were giving to pupils in our own subject areas. It became clear during that year that many of the issues and concerns which were raised were common to all of us. It seemed, then, a logical next step to see if it might be possible for us to work in collaboration with each other by taking a theme which could form the basis of classroom work in a number of different curriculum areas with one class. For one thing, we thought that this might provide a way of making the writing tasks on which pupils were engaged more meaningful.

Some of Cory's R.E. pupils had, in the previous term, produced some fascinating and surprising independent group-reports on 'prejudice' which had impressed all of us. Fay had noticed at the time how much of what they had said related closely to work that her History pupils were doing on the rise of Fascism. This was our 'way in'. We decided that the Second World War, and the 'Home Front' in particular, could form the basis of a cross-curricular investigation. The English, History and R.E. departments decided that they could modify their third year programmes of work accordingly. The Home Economics department then became drawn in and the Maths department agreed to give what help they could. We chose 3L because most of us in the working group actually taught that class.

We held a series of planning sessions. Because of the usual constraints of the timetable, we had to keep some of our ambitions in check. For example, team-teaching wasn't going to be an option for us but we thought that there would be sufficient flexibility for us at least to co-ordinate the work that was going to be undertaken in the different subject areas. In practice this seemed to work quite sensibly. In our different subject areas we tackled, or began to tackle, different aspects of our chosen theme and the pupils seemed to be aware that the link was a meaningful one. In R.E., Cory looked at the moral issues connected with the causes of the Second World War and went on to look at the positions held by people in the German churches, considering the idea of 'courage' from the perspective of 'ordinary people'. In History, Fay concentrated on the social issues arising from a study of the Home Front, looking at how people lived and the kinds of pressures and difficulties they faced. In English, pupils read and talked about war poetry and *The Diary of Anne Frank*, using these and the stimuli provided by the other subject areas as the basis for much of their work. The Home Economics department joined in by looking at what the Home Front meant to people in terms of diet and living conditions. These were the starting points. There were many obvious areas of overlap in all this, but in the event we were all surprised at just how much the learning spilled over from one subject area into another.

Needless to say, there were difficulties. Originally, we'd tried to organise our new programme into a fairly tight schedule. In the event, for all sorts of reasons, not the least of which was the pupils' enthusiasm, the work went on over the best part of a term! It only needs one teacher to be ill in a scheme like this for the plans to go haywire — particularly if another teacher is dependent on what that teacher is doing. We should have allowed for this. Perhaps our planning was even too tight in some respects.

Although we'd begun with some very vague ideas about how the written work generated by this programme might be varied from the 'norm', it wasn't until we actually began to work through the scheme that this became clearer. Perhaps we needed to see how the pupils responded? We certainly benefited from their ideas and advice. Looking back, it is really surprising how many different kinds of writing opportunities were provided for, and chosen by, the pupils. They weren't always what we had planned.

In R.E., for example, pupils made up their own questionnaire in order to find out more about prejudices which exist nowadays and to compare the situation with that which existed in Germany before the rise of Hitler. Having distributed this to other pupils and to parents and teachers, they made use of the results in their Maths lessons, converting their data into graphical form before explaining and presenting what they had found. In History and in English, pupils made up their own strongly empathetic accounts of life during wartime, using information from other subject areas. Claire wrote her despatch from the Warsaw Ghetto:

'Morale is high, success low. Every attempt to escape from the Ghetto is a dangerous journey into the unknown. Many attempt but few make it. It's an unknown where death and hatred lurk, joy and sorrow, but also the good things in life — the fresh air, flowers and freedom may lie just around the corner. Many people risk their lives in order that one person can see what is on the outside — to see that there is life beyond the barbed wire, a life that is good and full of promise, a life worth fighting for. The bravery of these people must be relayed to the world.'

Catherine described school life in wartime:

'We go to school which starts at eight and finishes at half-past three because we have a blackout at six. If we have anything to do where light is required we have to get it done by six … Every day in school the attendance becomes less and less. What with the dead and the ones sent to the country, the school is less than half of what it was before the war started. The teaching staff has been drastically cut back, what with male teachers joining up and the women training to be nurses, we only have three teachers — an old male Science teacher, a female English teacher who doubles up for History and Geography as well and a female Maths teacher who isn't really a Maths teacher but a secretary to an accountant who is now in the army.'

Alyson thought about what might have happened had Britain been invaded:

'I cannot go to the library for I am a Jew and cannot possess a library card. I am not allowed to go to school. I am not allowed out after eight o'clock for a curfew has been placed on us. I am not allowed to travel on any public transport for I wear the yellow Star of David which classifies me as a Jew. The only means of travel I am permitted to use is my own, my feet. I am surprised they have not stopped us breathing. Well, when I think about it, they have. Truckloads of Jews are shipped out of Britain to the concentration camps in Europe which have been re-opened.'

Many pupils took the opportunity to collect some primary source material of their own by interviewing relatives and other adults in the community about their experiences of the war and their memories of the Home Front. Michelle interviewed an older couple, Frank and Margaret:

'Margaret was living in Birmingham when Coventry was bombed, so they left and went to live in Maesteg for a year. After that they moved to Bridgend where they have been ever since. Her mother worked in the Royal Ordnance factory but as Margaret was only twelve she went to her local school. She had to carry her gas mask with her every day, but it was never used except for practices. They did, however, have to learn how to use a stirrup pump and there was always a fire drill …'

We all felt that it was very important that, from the start, the pupils in 3L should have some sense, not only of the direction of the work, but also of some control over it. At an early stage we asked the class how they felt that the work they were doing could be best used. It was the pupils themselves who suggested a display — originally for other third year pupils but eventually for their parents, too. As soon as this outcome had been established, the pupils began to expand their ambitions. A few short play-scenes had been generated by groups of pupils dealing with different aspects of life on the Home Front in Ystrad Mynach. These eventually formed the basis for the centrepiece of the final display — an hour-long play (with music!)

written and performed entirely by the pupils themselves. The play, *Family at War*, dealt with a whole range of the issues which the pupils' work on the Home Front had raised:

Mary: I heard that the GI's are coming up from Porthcawl!

1st girl: Great! We can get some stockings, and they've always got gum with them . . .

2nd girl: Yeah, but you know they always cause trouble with the boys!

1st girl: Who cares about the boys when we're going to get nylon stockings and chewing gum?!

Mary: Well, the others'll only get them first if we don't go in . . .'

Several teachers outside our group commented that the play itself, dealing with that particular subject matter, demonstrated more evidence of real learning than any number of filled exercise books could have done. The performance of the play, the display of pupils' work and the evidence and artifacts which they'd uncovered were given an added dimension by the contemporary refreshments: authentic wartime-recipe cakes which the pupils had prepared in Home Economics and served to the guests, together with Camp coffee, made with dried milk and saccharin!

It's true to say that what eventually emerged from this investigation was quite different from what we'd originally envisaged, despite our very careful planning and preparation. Looking back, we probably underestimated 3L's capacity to make decisions and organise work for themselves, given a reasonable level of stimulus and support. We certainly underestimated the extent to which subject boundaries would need to be (and were) broken down. All subject areas had a contribution to make — particularly in the case of the play.

The pupils' enthusiasm and commitment to the work ensured that the project was a success from their point of view. But we as a group of teachers learned a great deal from the experience. One of us wrote, afterwards:

'I feel that I've learned a lot. It's made me realise that a school day is made up of many disparate experiences for young people, that sometimes we as teachers can help bring these experiences together. It also affords us the opportunity of working with colleagues in a meaningful way.'

Finding that our concerns about writing and learning were, invariably, shared concerns led us into this Project. Perhaps what we've learned from it most of all is that it's more helpful to tackle those concerns together and not in subject-bound isolation.

Denise Hallam, Olwyn Hazleton, Judith Jones, Fay Swain, Jan Thomas, John Thornton and Cory Williams
Lewis Girls' Comprehensive School, Ystrad Mynach, Mid Glamorgan

Developing a language policy

A Primary school's collegiate approach

February

I gave a talk to the staff about word processing. Various handouts were distributed, including 'What we need when we write' from *About Writing, National Writing Project Newsletter 2* (see p 82).

Two word processing packages, *Alpha* and *Folio*, were demonstrated to those interested, and I arranged weekly lunch-time computer workshops to give staff an opportunity to exchange ideas and develop computer expertise.

April

There was a one-day school closure for staff INSET with the morning session devoted to language, particularly writing. Language resources, some borrowed from the LEA Language Resource Base, were displayed. My introductory talk provided an overview of current research into children's writing and addressed key issues such as *'What is writing?' 'Why do we write?' 'Who do we write for?' 'How can we help children to become writers?' 'The development of writing; how can word processing aid writing development?'* and *'How do teachers respond to children's writing?'* I tried to move the emphasis away from the product towards recognition of the process by which that product is reached.

The staff then divided into three groups with the theme 'Shared classroom practice'. 'Questions and practice' from *About Writing, National Writing Project Newsletter 4* (see p 83) was used as a discussion document.

Writing itself can be an invaluable point of contact between teachers and a focus for discussion and co-operation. The following account from a Primary school describes how one meeting on the subject of writing and micros mushroomed into a continuing dialogue, and led to the development of a whole school policy.

After a term's secondment to study word processing in the Primary school, Liz Neville returned to her post as language co-ordinator in January 1987. At a meeting of the school's senior management team it was decided that there was a need for new curriculum policy statements. Language was to be the first priority and Liz kept a diary.

Suppose that we, as individuals or as members of a group in a school, turned our attention to writing. What would we want to get clear in our minds? Here are seven *Key Ideas* about writing which apply to anybody who writes, not just to children writing in school. They are attempts to answer the question: what is natural behaviour for writers? In other words: what do writers do? what do they need? Writers means all of us who, some time in our lives, write for a purpose important to us.

WHAT
WE
NEED
WHEN
WE
WRITE

DRAFTING: Almost all writers need to work on something until it's near enough right. Sometimes the drafting occurs in the head, sometimes on the page. The more important or difficult a piece of writing is, the more likely that it will have to be approached several times, with accumulating degrees of success. Satisfaction comes from a product that you are pleased with.

WRITERS AS ASSESSORS: The development of a critical sense, the ability to get outside your own or someone else's product, to make judgements, is an essential half of the reflexivity between creation and criticism. Writers need it.

COLLABORATION: The process of interaction, conversation, mutual support and criticism, grants orientation and critical space to the writer, as well as the benefit of another's ideas. While collaboration should never become enforced committee meetings, and while writers need very often to be left to get on with the job, there are also times when there is simply no way forward without it.

UNDERLYING ORDER: Even when a piece of writing seems to have gone badly wrong, there are reasons for that which can be discovered. What appears at first glance to be random and chaotic, turns out at second and third glance to have an organisation to it.

DEVELOPMENT: All writers have come from somewhere and are going towards somewhere else, as long as they keep writing. Going towards somewhere else does not necessarily mean somewhere good; some developments are blind alleys or red herrings. But writers need a sense of personal history, of having moved, improved, in order to sustain their impetus.

REAL PURPOSE, REAL AUDIENCE, REAL MODES OF DISTRIBUTION: Almost all writers need all three of these. Some diarists and mystics need only two, or even one. For the mainstream of writers, all three are life blood.

WRITERS NEED TEACHERS WHO WRITE: Like learners of other important human activites, writers need to see that more experienced people, people from whom they learn, write too, and that they too sometimes find it hard: to them too it offers rewards, pains and challenges.

Would you agree with these Key Ideas? Agree with some but not with others? Want to modify the wording? Add Key Ideas which have been omitted? Combine them where they seem to overlap?

Here are seven statements about what has often happened in schools in relation to each of the Key Ideas.

The majority of writing tasks in schools are once-for-all efforts: fairground shooting games where you only have one shot. The pressures of timetable, curriculum content, teacher's nervousness about output, mean that the chance to work on and take control of a piece, to get the confidence resulting from that, comes rarely. Even when teachers are persuaded of the value of drafting, it is hard to know how to get beyond thinking of drafting merely as 'rough copy' and 'neat copy'.

Because teachers are the only assessors of pupils' writing, the critical sense in the pupil dies through lack of exercise. Also, the unmitigated obligation to create, to offer up products for the judgement of a superior other, means that many young writers are constantly over-exposed and vulnerable.

Most writing in school is done in solitary confinement. The writer, imprisoned with the task, seeks release in the perfunctory, the minimum acceptable.

We, the teachers, are dismayed, confused and guilty about the superficial failings of our pupils' work. Out of a sense of duty, we resort to repetitive and negative attention to the symptoms of technical failure, rather than trying to comprehend causes and patterns.

Most writers in school live in an eternal present, with no feeling of growth. Writing is a daily duty like teeth-cleaning, not a long-term progress of understanding and competence.

The only purpose for most pieces of writing done in school is that the teacher has requested them; the only audience is the teacher in the role of assessor; the only mode of distribution is one return journey from pupil to teacher and back.

Most teachers never write for or in front of their pupils.

John Richmond
SCDC National Writing Project

These statements are intended to present a 'worst-case' picture. You may be affronted by some of them, feeling that your practice is more advanced than they suggest. Others may strike a chord of agreement in you. In either case, a worthwhile task would be:

to discuss approaches to writing which try to resolve the dilemma produced by the gap between the Key Ideas and the 'what's wrong now' statements. These approaches might be a part of your work already, or they might still be uncertain possibilities which need clearer formulation and then trying out. In the course of this discussion, you may find yourself planning (or revising) a policy for writing in your school.

Questions & Practice

Planning for a more developed writing curriculum, often involves looking at ways in which children's classroom experiences can reflect the everyday uses of writing outside the classroom. Some relevant questions might be:

What do we use writing for?

Every day we use writing to
- remember things
- organise ideas
- reconstruct information
- reflect on experience
- communicate with others
- clarity ideas
- report on events
- share opinions
- entertain
- persuade – and more

When children are asked why they write they sometimes show that they're not at all clear about the purposes of writing

Teacher says so.
So we don't get told off.
Punishment.

But it can be
A way of working
- lists, jottings, diagrams, drafts
- journals, logs, notes, poems
- A means of reflection
- Preparation for non-written outcomes
- radio broadcasts, talks, plays
- Communication
- letters, accounts, pamphlets, stories, explanations

It's a natural thing to write.
To take something off our minds.

We write because it's fun.

We write to enjoy it and for other people to enjoy what we write.
(Class of 10 year olds)

Who do we write for? Who reads it?

We write for
- ourselves
- family
- friends
- acquaintances
- unknown others.

There are often clear differences between classroom and school writing

The person who writes the stuff and the teacher are the only ones to read it. (Geoffrey 15 years)

What you write is up to you if you are at home, and if you are at school it is up to the teacher what you write about. (Carol 9 years)

But it can be
- a personal record
- work logs as a basis for discussion with the teacher
- letters to friends or others
- explanations to parents about work
- books or information sheets for other children or adults
- class or school newspapers

I like writing because I sometimes get replies.

It brings back memories.

I write because people like to have news of you.

To show other children.
(Class of 8 year olds)

What happens to writing when it's finished?

Writing can be
- thrown away when it has done its job
- replied to
- published for others to read
- kept as a valued memento
- used as a basis for discussion
- sent as a message – and more

Sometimes children see writing as an automatic activity

Most of the time we copy out of books. (Vanya 11 years)
So we are not given text books. (Mark 14 years)
We write so the teacher can tell us our mistakes. (Steven 12 years)

But it can be
- displayed in draft and finished form
- collected or published in anthologies, books or magazines
- used for discussion or planning
- sent to other classes or schools
- taken home to be discussed or developed
- put in libraries
- kept as part of a selected record of progress.

So I can look back and enjoy the stories and bits of writing I have done in the last years. (Anna 9 years)
Writing's O.K. It gives me something material. I can say 'I've done this'. (Julia 15 years)
I liked it when we wrote the books for the infants. (Mario 11 years)

What makes for effective writing?

To be effective writers we need
- a reason for writing
- time and space
- a choice of writing materials
- a choice of approach
- response to what we've written
- experience of different forms of writing.

Children sometimes find the demands of classroom writing too much

It makes my hand hurt. (Kim 6 years)
I don't like it when the bell goes and I haven't finished. (Seren 8 years)
Writing's boring. (Alex 11 years)

But it can
- form part of an agreed programme of work over a period of time
- arise from topics chosen by the writer
- result from collaboration with other writers in the classroom
- be a series of experiments with new strategies and forms.

It takes time and care to make a really good piece of work.
All you need is good concentration and to learn a lot, have patience and a bit of peace and quiet.
(Class of 9 year olds)

What are the different formats for writing?

Writing appears as
- jottings, drawings, notes
- typescript
- word processor printout
- handwritten notes and letters
- entries in journals or log books
- draft manuscripts
- books, newspapers, magazines
- pamphlets and advertisements.

Exercise books are often the only place children write

Miss keeps all our full books in the cupboard. (Gemma 7 years)
I like it when I've filled up my book. (Anthony 7 years)

But writing can also appear in
- loose leaf folders
- collections of individual or class work
- journals, special scrapbooks
- books written for others
- information packs, guidesheets
- diagrams or charts
- wall displays showing techniques of drafting or planning

I write so I can make things like maps. (Ellen 9 years)
I write in my secret diary. (George 10 years)

How do we develop writing capabilities

Writing development can be promoted by
- having the chance to experiment
- talking about writing
- helpful response
- being readers of our own and others' writing
- having some experience of different techniques and strategies for planning
- revising and editing
- looking back on writing over a period of time to notice progress and problems.

Children can be sensitive about the way their writing is treated

I do my best but its still wrong. (Diana 13 years)

But development can happen through
- offering ways of responding to the content of writing
- children having a vocabulary with which they can talk about writing
- developing strategies for organising and editing writing
- talking about drafts before, during and after composition
- teachers writing alongside children
- having a chance to collaborate over writing
- keeping files of work and discussing them at regular intervals
- allowing children to ask questions
- making the purpose and forms of writing more explicit.

I like to work with Martin best. He writes good stories. (James 9 years)

One sure way of developing a writing curriculum is through the shared experience of good classroom practice. You may like to use these ideas as a basis for discussion.

. . . or compile a list of classroom activities which have helped children to write for a variety of purposes or for different readers . . . or you could start by asking children their views about why they write.

Eve Bearne – based on contributions from project working groups

At the end of the INSET session it was decided that:

- Opportunities for drafting were to be developed throughout the school, varying according to age groups.

- The use of the micro as a language resource would be further developed.

- Working parties would be set up to consider aspects of the language curriculum.

May

Staff response was very positive and all members volunteered to serve on language working parties which met one evening per week after school. The head requested that we consider writing first.

Finding it very difficult to focus on the various aspects of writing which needed to be included in our discussions, I produced a flow chart to provide some structure. We divided into three groups of four, each group taking responsibility for particular areas as defined by the chart.

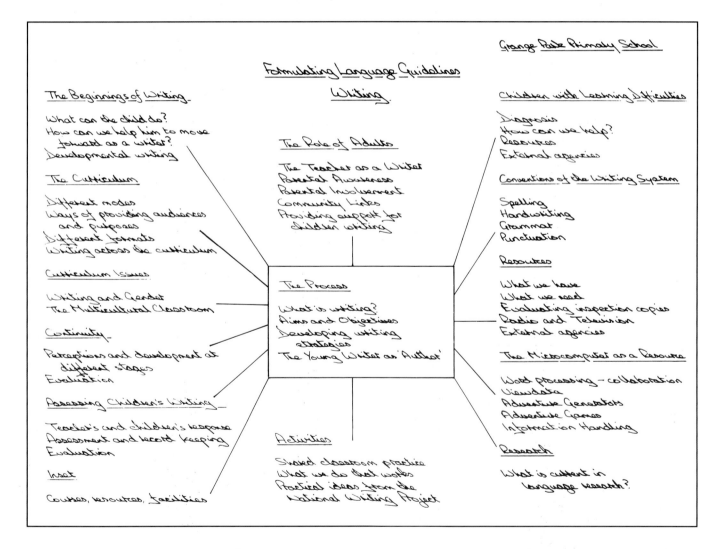

June

The working parties continued to meet weekly. I provided discussion documents, relevant handouts and general guidance. Working party notes were given to me. We became bogged down with spelling, so invited the LEA language advisory teacher in to give a talk at a staff meeting.

At a meeting of language postholders in Enfield, I described our collegiate approach to the development of a language policy. This promoted much discussion and sharing of ideas. The postholders found, as one might expect, that lack of time is a great constraint.

At the end of June, due to pressure of time, our language working parties moved on to consider oracy.

October

I began to formulate Draft Writing Guidelines, liaising with the head. Meanwhile, working parties continued to meet to discuss other aspects of the language curriculum.

Throughout the school there seemed to be much more informal discussion about writing. Members of staff were trying out new ideas and evaluating them. Children in many classes were writing collaboratively using a word processor. A workshop for parents was held to explain the educational philosophy behind the use of word processors in the classroom and to give the parents an opportunity to write collaboratively using them.

January 1988 and on . . .

I am still compiling the Draft Writing Guidelines. These include aims, objectives, teaching strategies, classroom activities, use of resources, ways to ensure progression and continuity, methods of record keeping, and aspects of assessment and evaluation. Some sections of the writing policy have been completed and are being implemented, but the writing of the guidelines is taking longer than I anticipated. There continues to be much consultation with the head who is very supportive of my role.

When our Draft Writing Guidelines are fully implemented, they will be monitored and evaluated. Revision will be needed in response not only to our internal evaluation but also to changing circumstances, local and national initiatives and research findings. I see the process of developing a language policy as a corporate venture, one which is professionally valuable for all concerned and very much a continuing activity.

Liz Neville, Grange Park Primary School, London Borough of Enfield

Work experience

A focus for Secondary curriculum development

Work experience has come to be accepted now in our school as a regular feature of the curriculum for fourth and fifth year pupils. I believe its importance in the learning process needs to be emphasised and more done to increase the number of real experiences for pupils. The world of work will become many pupils' everyday environment once they leave full-time education and the preparation for this, which includes work experience or in some cases work 'shadowing', is the responsibility of all teachers, although the main focus at the moment is often in Personal and Social Education, Tutorial and Careers programmes. However, I believe that there is room for work experience to become integrated into the curriculum in more ways than this and much of my Writing Project work so far has been an attempt to show that this is possible.

Current curriculum developments encourage (even instruct) us to put work experience in a prominent place. For instance, TVEI demands that experience of

The development of links between school and the world outside, with the consequent breaking down of curriculum divisions, opens up a further range of possibilities for cross-curricular approaches to writing. In the following article, a Secondary school teacher explains the important role that work experience can play in the curriculum, and describes some of the opportunities it can offer.

work be part of the core and it is possible for modular courses to revolve around it. CPVE, with its emphasis on vocational education, also relates strongly to a work experience element. A year ago I decided that I wanted to explore perceptions about work and working life and made arrangements for one of my English sets to undertake a week of work experience. This was work experience for me too, as doing what is traditionally done by a Careers teacher caused a few headaches for me and not a few raised eyebrows from colleagues. It offered valuable insights as I spent hour after hour making (often fruitless) phone calls and writing seemingly endless numbers of letters. But it was worth it as I made contact with a number of personnel officers and managers, and was able to explain my objectives to them.

The next stage was to prepare a booklet with the help of the pupils to guide them in their observations, asking them to research their workplaces and the writing that went on there. Compiling this work experience journal offered the opportunity of tackling a wide range of writing tasks, demanding different styles and directed at different audiences and purposes. One of the important factors involved in finding out about work is to discover the ways in which it compares with or is different from school; to challenge understanding of our own working life by analysing a day at school.

Another kind of writing involved perceptions: what will it be like going to work? What will be different from school? What is involved in doing certain jobs? I was horrified by my own ignorance and impressed by the depth in which some pupils described jobs in which they were interested. However, the work experience group tried to focus on their placement choices and children's expectations and perceptions of the jobs they would be experiencing. More fascinating insights emanated from the questions pupils asked at work about writing. We don't always know what kinds of writing go on at work and how school writing might be relevant.

On return from work experience, the pupils used their journals to construct guides for other pupils, combining factual information gleaned from the workplace with their own reflections and some account of the work involved. This has been typed and duplicated and is now available to fourth years in the Careers library. Some of the pupils decided to produce a booklet for third years, giving advice about choosing options, and were rewarded by seeing the booklet used as a class resource for third year Careers lessons. The other main piece of writing was a daily log — here there was enormous variation in response. I hope these logs will help form another booklet for future generations of pupils.

There are many possibilities for work in a variety of curriculum areas. At Testwood our plans are the result of negotiation, a lot of enthusiasm and goodwill, and invaluable help from agencies like the School Curriculum Industry Partnership and the Schools Industry Liaison Officers' Network. Teachers from subject areas which have a demand for work experience in GCSE courses: Integrated Humanities, English, Business Information Studies, Careers, Personal and Social Education, Applied Biology and Home and Family are all involved. It was agreed that work experience should be central to the Integrated Humanities' 'World of work' module which would become part of the TVEI core. (It is already part of the compulsory core.) The two courses which involve most writing — English and Integrated Humanities — are working together to ensure that there isn't duplication or overlap and that each subject designs its modules in collaboration with the other.

Of course, 'World of work' modules can incorporate more ways of stimulating pupils' interest in and understanding of work. English activities extend into creative and imaginative elements and introduce a wide range of literature. Integrated Humanities has its own path through case studies and simulations. Cross-curricular fertilisation is being encouraged by the deployment of two English teachers into Humanities to explore further links between the subjects. Work experience placements are being organised by members of all interested departments.

For ensuing years, it is hoped that staff from other areas of the curriculum will join in and introduce appropriately structured work related to the 'World of work'.

One of the most valuable aspects of this cross-curricular experiment was the way in which it established teams of teachers working together across traditional boundaries. Both staff and pupils have also been made aware of the links between curriculum areas and the equal relevance of different approaches to writing. At a social level, all the teachers involved visited pupils in their workplaces. This was an eye-opening yet subtle slice of staff development that engendered enormous interest and enthusiasm. The co-operation and goodwill of the team (often under pressure) were remarkable. There is a very clear message: if teachers work together they can offer the pupils a wholeness and a balance in looking at their lives after school. If work experience is central to pupils' learning and writing experiences we can see what may be built on this core.

Liz Vicary, Testwood School, Totton, Southampton

With particular thanks to John Archer, Derek Hiscocks, Don Tremayne and the pupils of Testwood School

---

For discussion

How can writing form the basis for joint activities? Colleagues might like to use this diagram as a framework for considering ways of extending the writing curriculum offered to pupils. What are the possibilities for:

Working Together

Across the curriculum
— joint programmes

?

?

?

With others
— parents, employees, the community

?

?

?

With colleagues
— developing policy

?

?

?

With pupils
— collective enterprises

?

?

?

What benefits can be gained?

Teachers' comments

'In our Middle school I set about planning a pastoral care programme which would gradually draw in the rest of the team of teachers and show that pastoral care activities could operate in the same way as any curricular programme; that issues of personal and social development can be explored at the same time as developing oral and writing abilities. The theme was "Our identity" and each class contributed some work to a joint newspaper.'

'There was a wide range in the quality of the writing and presentation in the final magazine. I didn't feel greatly perturbed about this as it was the process that had been most important. A lot of learning had taken place in the compilation of the reports. Classes had to work collaboratively, group and class discussion was necessary, organisational and practical skills were called upon and all aspects of language were practised and developed.'

'We took the chance of using some in-service days to look at how we could introduce information technology into more curriculum areas. It was helpful to use writing as a focus because it's needed for every subject, particularly now that GCSE means more emphasis on writing in different ways. Our difficulties were the usual ones — people's fears of computers and technical jargon, which I hope we've managed to deal with by "hands on" experience; time — a real problem — not just for discussion but for actually getting the machinery into the classroom; access to the computers — our specialist computer staff have been very helpful, but I know of some schools where the machinery is locked away and only used for computer studies. We feel we're on the way and certainly we've got a great deal out of desktop publishing for the school newspaper and class publications; databases for information gathering, storage and retrieval; opportunities for talk when pupils are using simulations or games. And the pupils do seem to be more positive about writing.'

'I asked my colleagues about the writing requirements of GCSE exams. Examples from Art, CDT, Science and Maths revealed that a broader range of writing is now needed. Their replies included:

- *reflective uses of writing and self-assessment*
- *use of technical vocabulary*
- *analytical writing (research documentation)*
- *writing as a response to given material*
- *argumentative or opinion writing (based on factual and deductive evidence — e.g. Maths)*
- *interpretations of diagrams; graphs, tables*
- *justifying and exploring ideas*
- *observation and descriptive writing (e.g. Science experiments)*
- *hypothesising; drawing conclusions*
- *giving information*
- *note-making and summarising*
- *using writing to help make investigations'*

'In our Primary school we thought a good way to look at writing would be to collect examples of children's work and discuss them. It was amazing how we found good points which we'd overlooked in the classroom. We had some lively discussions about spelling etc. but this led us on to looking at reading and the kinds of reading materials we offer the children, including our classroom displays and reading scheme. We've decided to have a good look at the books, both information and stories, that we have in school; to think carefully about whether they offer positive images of our children's home cultures; to look at ways we can help children read for different purposes and, most importantly, to try to encourage children to read for fun.'

Summary

The accounts in this section acknowledge frankly the difficulties often experienced when colleagues want to develop joint activities:

- Time is needed to establish common ground and to develop a shared way of talking about writing and learning.

- Emphasis on the content of a particular subject area can make for difficulties; when working with colleagues in other departments in a Secondary school it's probably more profitable to find a broad theme from which all subjects can benefit.

- There are sometimes worries about parents' or other teachers' attitudes to new approaches to writing; these need to be discussed openly to find ways of explaining the purposes and benefits of joint activities.

Ways of dealing with the constraints can be found by:

- asking teachers with particular expertise to contribute to an activity

- using in-service sessions to plan activities or to discuss developing new policies

- finding areas where GCSE students might use a common enquiry for coursework in different subjects

- using existing programmes like Personal and Social Education, work experience, CPVE or TVEI courses to plan jointly

- starting the ball rolling by consulting colleagues about the writing requirements of their subject areas as a basis for finding common ground

- seeing how the introduction of new technology or a review of reading policy might be aided by looking at the place of writing in learning

- finding ways of involving the community or employers both as a resource for writing and as an audience

- encouraging pupils to see how writing can be used to fulfil their own purposes in all areas of the curriculum as well as being used to communicate with others

An overview

Write across the curriculum
Summing up and pointing forward

If you write yourself, you will certainly have had the experience of not knowing exactly what you thought until you started to write, or of realising half-way through that you'd started in the wrong place anyway. Such experiences, and others like them, show us that writing is a powerful tool for organising and developing thought, and the more you write yourself, the more this is apparent — one reason why teachers in the National Writing Project are encouraged to write.

Contrast this tentative, flexible, exploratory sort of writing with a traditional classroom writing situation in almost any subject, when a teacher gives information orally or in note form and then asks the learner to reproduce the information as the end point of the activity, ostensibly to provide evidence of learning having been achieved. Granted, the injunction 'in your own words' is sometimes added, but how effective is this when the words of the original speaker or writer exert such a potent influence because of their status? More importantly, the task set is just that, an imposition of someone else's account of the subject matter. The same applies to getting information from books, which sometimes consists of performing the function of a photocopying machine, only not so well. In these cases, the 'new' writing context is almost identical to the original and, moreover, its purpose and audience are rarely specified. There is no scope here for learners effectively to demonstrate their learning. The timing of the writing, at the end of the activity, precludes the further development and refinement of ideas which drafting would have allowed and reinforces the mistaken assumption that writing is only useful after learning has taken place.

At worst, a straitjacket of stylised conventional structure (method/result/ conclusion in Science, for example) may be imposed on the writing of a whole class so that individual learning by personal engagement with the experience is actually inhibited. More worrying still, pupils learn to follow such linguistic conventions without ever making the connection with their own learning. Definitions and specialist vocabulary may be manipulated with a dexterity which effectively masks failure to comprehend the concepts to which they refer. It is perhaps a fear of exposing the incompleteness of their pupils' learning which accounts for the reluctance of some teachers to break away from the formulaic writing which has become hallowed by tradition in their subjects.

Most teachers, if challenged, would identify, in all school subjects, a range of cognitive skills which they hope to develop in their pupils (hypothesis, empathy, classification and so on), and yet the writing activities set by some teachers cover only a few of these areas. The ways in which writing may be used along the way to learning, rather than as evidence of its completion, are rarely exploited. Indeed, there are some subject areas where writing is not considered an appropriate means of learning at all.

What is needed, then, is a range of writing activities which are truly effective in encouraging learning because they demand the reorganisation of knowledge by learners themselves, and allow both teachers and learners to make the learning process as visible as it can be. Writing of this kind can be a sort of window into the learner's mind. Their writing is, after all, the most immediately accessible evidence we have of what is going on inside our

Margaret Wallen, one of the co-ordinators of the Dorset Writing Project, revisits the issues raised throughout this pack of materials and offers a collection of practical suggestions to support writing and learning in different curriculum areas. These ideas are not new. You may recognise activities which you have already adopted as part of your regular classroom practice. They reflect the varieties of routes which teachers have found to promote successful learning.

pupils' heads. For the learners, too, writing should provide a record at each stage of learning which may be consulted, reviewed and adapted over a period of time.

Here are some practical suggestions, from a variety of sources, for:

- general strategies which enable pupils to initiate their own writing and become actively involved in their own learning by using their existing knowledge as a starting point

- other strategies which help them to maintain impetus, control and self-awareness while they are writing and so remain engaged with the learning process

- some activities which promote learning through writing in a direct way

As subject specialists we can adapt these activities to suit our particular area of study, but all of these suggestions are applicable to every part of the curriculum. The fact that some are currently employed by only a few teachers is due to our limited assumptions about the nature and purpose of writing, not to any inherent limitations of its potential as a tool for learning. What is 'appropriate' to a subject must surely include what is useful to promoting learning within it. The activities may often be undertaken in groups as well as by individuals, and may be considered to be relevant to a wide range of age and ability. It is worth trying a number of different approaches, since pupils seem to learn in different ways and may find some more helpful than others.

1 Strategies for initiating writing

Writing to introduce a topic

Ask pupils to write in a personal and expressive way about the topic in response to oral questions. These should encourage them to identify what they already know, to make connections between their experience and the topic, to place it in a broader context and to express opinions and attitudes. Examples of questions:

What do you like and dislike about . . .?
What is the most difficult part of this topic?
What facts do you know about . . .?
Write your own definition of . . .

Responses may be shared and from this a consensus will emerge which will show both teacher and learners their starting points.

Framing your own questions

Ask pupils to write down the questions about the topic to which they would really like to have answers. They can then plan how they will find these answers. This may involve, in particular subjects, creating a hypothesis and working out how to test it, or simply classifying areas for further research from reference material.

Using diagrams

All sorts of diagrams (eg drawings, flow charts, tables, webs etc) may be used by pupils to map out the area covered by the topic and the connections between its parts. The significance of any one part within the whole is then more likely to be grasped, and priorities may be selected more effectively from all of the possible starting points. The diagram also acts as a long-term plan to which reference may be made at later stages of the writing.

Brainstorming

Give pupils a limited time to write down, just as they think of them and without any attempt at ordering, as many words, phrases and images as they can, which are connected with the topic. These may then be shared as a class and common themes identified and ordered by the pupils themselves, perhaps by using some of the techniques described above.

Visualising (for expressive writing)

Young children may be asked to close their eyes and make pictures in their mind as the teacher 'walks them through' a scene by asking them what they see, hear, etc, until they build up a detailed mental picture on which they can base their story or poem. With very young children, the scene may be actually drawn before writing begins and may then act as a plan for the writing.

2 Ways of working which help to maintain impetus, control and self-awareness during writing

Teacher modelling writing

Teachers can help to make the writing process and its connection with learning explicit in their own behaviour as writers. They can demonstrate to their pupils (using a blackboard, O.H.P. or flip chart) how they use writing to sort out ideas, make hypotheses, plan actions, ask questions, etc.

Drafting

Pupils may be given the opportunity to make as many attempts as they need at a piece of writing. A writing folder may be more appropriate than an exercise book, and some of the 'interim' writing can be thrown away once it has served its purpose of clarifying ideas. Teachers may, once again, act as models of this process.

Conferencing

Pupils may be given the opportunity to discuss work in progress or future plans for writing with the teacher, rather than waiting until it is finished. The structuring of the writing is made explicit and the teacher is able to intervene productively.

Collaborative writing

Two or more pupils may work together to produce a piece of writing. The learning which emerges from purposeful talk will result in insights and the development of ideas which they might not have achieved individually, and can make explicit the purpose and organisation of the piece.

Response partners

Pairs of children who respect each other take turns to comment constructively on each other's writing, enabling the writer to refine the piece in response to the demands and reactions of a real audience.

Publication for real audiences

There is abundant evidence of the motivation, which a real audience may produce in the writer, to produce high quality work.

3 Writing activities which specifically promote learning

Learning logs

Give pupils a book in which they write for themselves, in any way they wish, about their current learning, in one or more subjects. This might include questions, speculations, statements, plans or diagrams. The idea is to give them a space to sort out in private what they are thinking and understanding about your lessons, including areas of confusion or anxiety. If they show it to you, you may respond by writing a comment or asking questions which encourage further thought, as well as gaining valuable information about your pupils' learning.

Problem-solving

Pupils identify the problem themselves, or respond to one identified by the teacher. Writing is used for a number of purposes both during and after the exercise, e.g. planning, speculating, recording, defining, explaining, reporting.

Explaining a topic to someone else

Some formats we are using in the Dorset project include beginners' guides to the school library or to a hobby, and guides to the school for new pupils, but the writing may also be presented more informally, read aloud to the class or as an assembly, for example, or as a report on current investigations and future plans.

Writing directions/instructions

Pupils may write instructions for others to follow, to construct a model or to perform a sequence of actions, for example. They should be tested and refined until they are a completely effective communication.

Rewriting a text for a different audience

Pupils may be asked to rewrite a text by another writer on the subject currently being studied, so that it is suitable for a specified audience, for example a younger child or one who doesn't know certain items of vocabulary. In this way, the pupil's grasp of the essential concepts will be revealed.

Writing in response to a text

Texts by other writers may also be used with older pupils to encourage active response to the ideas they contain. Pupils write directly on to a copy of the text or on to a separate piece of paper as they read it, making comments, asking questions, numbering points, underlining parts, making comparisons, and so on.

Note-making

This is a complex and demanding activity which involves a number of different skills, may take several different forms and so needs to be taught. The different purposes served by notes (subdivision, locating relevant information, making connections with other material, etc.) need to be made explicit: pupils will not just 'pick them up'. A range of useful techniques needs to be demonstrated on real texts and time must be allowed for pupils to try them out on their current reading matter.

Modelling

A further development of some of the above ideas or an alternative form of note-making is the use of diagrams of all sorts to represent comprehension of a text by another writer. Examples include maps, matrices, hierarchies, graphs or time lines which involve the translation of written information into another form using less writing and more graphic material. There is clearly an overlap here with a range of techniques which may be used to develop 'higher order' reading abilities, and this reminds us that reading and writing development are interdependent.

Constructing questionnaires

This activity may be compared with writing directions/instructions (as above) in its need for precise, unambiguous writing for a specific audience. It also encourages the ordering of information into a logical sequence and the sorting of relevant and irrelevant items.

Writing in role

Ask pupils to assume the persona of, for example, a character in a novel, a historical figure, a famous scientist or the eye witness of a famous event, and write as if they were that person. Forms of writing used can be very varied and could include letters, diaries, speeches, newspaper reports, dialogues, interviews or advertisements. Pupils could also be asked to imagine that they are one constituent of a larger process[e.g. a molecule, a blood corpuscle or part of an engine, and describe the process from the point of view of that part.

Any approach which gives learners more control of their own writing and, by implication, of their own learning, also involves a change of role for the teacher. Time and patience, and a tolerance of false starts and blind alleys are needed by the teacher who allows learners to construct their own meaning through writing. It takes confidence and committed teachers to give their pupils this sort of opportunity.

Margaret Wallen, Dorset Writing Project Co-ordinator